D0451788

KACHINA TALES

FROM THE INDIAN PUEBLOS

Collected by Gene Meany Hodge

SUNSTONE PRESS

SANTA FE ◆ NEW MEXICO

The material in this book originally appeared in *The Kachinas Are Coming* by Gene Meany Hodge published by Bruce McAllister in 1936 and appears in this Sunstone Press edition by exclusive arrangement with The School of American Research, Santa Fe, New Mexico

© 1993 by The School of American Research

All Rights Reserved

No part of this book may be reproduced in any form or by any electronic or mechanical means including information storage and retrieval systems, without permission in writing from the publisher, except by a reviewer who may quote brief passages in a review.

Printed in the United States of America

Library of Congress Cataloging in Publication Data

Hodge, Gene Meany
    Kachina Tales from the Indian Pueblos / Collected by Gene Meany
Hodge. -- 1st ed.
        p. cm.
    "Material in this book originally appeared in The kachinas are
coming by Gene Meany Hodge published by Bruce McAllister in
1936"--Verso t.p.
      Includes bibliographical references (p. 64)
      ISBN: 0-86534-184-2 : $8.95
      1. Kachina dolls. 2. Pueblo Indians--Religion and mythology.
3. Pueblo Indians--Legends. I. Hodge, Gene Meany. Kachinas are
coming. II. Title.
E99.P9H65 1993
398.2'089'974--dc20
                                       92-47271
                                            CIP

Published by   Sunstone Press
                    Post Office Box 2321
                    Santa Fe, New Mexico 87504-2321 / USA
                    (505) 988-4418 / *orders only* (800) 243-5644
                    FAX (505) 988-1025
                    www.sunstonepress.com

CONTENTS

INTRODUCTION

This collection, from authentic sources, of the folklore and myths of the American Indian was gathered by Gene Meany Hodge in the 1930s and centers around the sacred supernatural personages of the Pueblo Indians called Kachinas (pronounced Kah-chee-nahs). They are represented by masked men in the dances and ceremonies practiced by the Indians and these masked men are in turn represented by effigies or dolls, made to resemble in costume, masks, ornaments and symbolism, the personages they are intended to depict. These objects are usually carved by the men during intervals in the performance of rites in the kivas (special ceremonial chambers) and are afterward given to the children.

Gene Meany Hodge wrote: "All in all the Kachinas are lovable and kindly supernaturals who bring rain and other blessings to the people. But if a man who is wearing a Kachina mask, thus impersonating the Kachina, is not pure of heart or fails in his trust, quick and dire punishment will be meted out to him, for the spirit of the Kachina is believed to be in the mask."

Although the origin of Kachinas is lost in time, they are probably as old as the American Indian people for whom they still exist. They have continued to be an integral part of their culture and mythology. According to Hopi legend, the Hopis and the Kachinas emerged together from the underworld and eventually settled in what is now eastern Arizona in the Southwestern part of the United States. In time, the Kachinas withdrew to the San Francisco Mountains. Zuni tradition tells of lost children who were transformed into Kachinas and live under the waters of a lake. In other legends from other tribes, Kachinas live in the clouds, in springs or other locations usually inaccessible to humans.

In all this varied mythology, however, there are certain similar details. Kachinas are frequently said to have left their human companions because people became indifferent to them and no longer respected them. In all the accounts, the Kachinas before leaving selected certain individuals to whom they entrusted their secrets and the knowledge of their rituals. It was these favored few who knew how to make the masks and costumes so that the Kachinas could be represented in the dances. They were also the ones who knew what rituals should be followed and when dances should be performed. All this made possible a continued if changed relationship between Kachina guides and humans

In addition to the dances, Kachina dolls are a highly visible reminder of the Kachinas. Originally these carved figures were used to teach children about the different Kachinas and what they represented. In today's world, however, they have become objects of trade and commerce. While at one time these figures could be bought only at trading posts or directly from Indians, Kachinas are now found in every shop that carries Native American crafts. Kachinas vary from very simple, even crudely carved forms to very complex, ornate ones.

Most dolls are carved from cottonwood. Originally organic paint and live evergreens were used for decoration. Noses, arms, and legs were carved or pegged into place. Feathers from various birds were also used as decoration. Today commercial paints are used, green yarn or plastic greenery is sometimes seen, especially in the lower priced dolls. Noses and arms may be glued on and legs no longer carved separately. Carved feathers or chicken feathers have become common since the feathers of certain birds can no longer be legally used. Kachinas vary in size from the very miniature of one to two inches to those of two feet in height or more.

While Kachinas are a part of the mythology of many different Indian tribes, they are more predominant among the Hopi and Zuni Indians of New Mexico and Arizona. The Hopis have the greatest number, well over 250 kachinas. Each Kachina is imbued with the spirit of an animal, bird, insect, plant, place, object, or person. This spirit determines the special function of the Kachina and the services it performs. For example, the Hopis have a Snow Kachina to whom they appeal for snow in the mountains so that there will be water in the spring. It is also thought that having snow will help the hunters track game animals. The Sun Kachina is important because many Indians, especially the Zunis, believe that the sun is the source of all life.

Kachinas have continued to play important roles in the lives of Indians. They are intermediaries between the actual world and the unseen world. They bring rain and have a part in the blessing of the crops. Some Kachinas aid pregnant women, others cure a variety of diseases. Dangers can be overcome with the help of the right Kachina and they are also used to admonish wrongdoers. In particular, children who are naughty or disrespectful can be made to change their behavior by being threatened by such a Kachina. Among the Hopi, Nataska seeks out naughty children; at Zuni, Atoshle is the ogre figure. The Pueblo Indians also have similar Kachinas. At Cochiti there are the River Men who come in the spring from the Rio Grande. They carry big sacks in which to take children who have misbehaved back to the river with them. The threat of this and the fear it brings is usually enough to encourage better conduct and a respectful attitude toward parents and other adults. In general, the Kachinas insure the physical and spiritual well-being of their followers.

The dances and the dolls are two aspects of Kachinas and the legends are a third. These legends or myths are a form of teaching and learning. They are also a form of historic preservation of a people and their beliefs. Thus, we find that each Kachina also has its legend, its story that helps people understand the use and truth behind the figure or image. Legends, of course, are a part of every culture, every ethnic and social group. Understanding a people's legends is a way of understanding them, understanding their history and their mores. Tradition as handed down in legends can be a decided factor in keeping a people as a living, functional entity.

The legends of the Kachinas are a unifying and cohesive force in the continuance of Native American social history. Buyers and collectors of Kachinas have an obligation to remember that each has a legend, a function and a place in the pantheon of Indian mythology. Knowing the legend makes the ownership of a Kachina more viable. It adds another dimension to the figure so that it has more meaning than that of a doll sitting on a shelf or table. Many of these legends can be found in this book. ❖

WHY KACHINAS WEAR EAGLE FEATHERS

KWAHU (EAGLE) KACHINA

Long ago a Zuni boy was set up on a cliff by witches. For four days he had nothing to eat.

This boy had a friend, Witch Boy, who asked him what he knew. He answered, "I do not know anything." So then the Witch Boy said, "I shall rub you all over with a black ant and then nothing can harm you." He did that, and then he took a hoop and jumped through it and turned into a chipmunk. He told the boy to do the same, and said it was easy and that he could turn himself back into a person whenever he wanted to.

So the boy did it. Then they went up a mountain to hunt. Witch Boy went ahead and told the other to wait while he went to look for birds' nests. Then he turned himself back into a person. He gave the hoop to the other boy and told him to turn himself back into a person too. This he did.

Then Witch Boy said, "Now, do you want me to teach you how to do it yourself, the way my mother taught me?"

But the other answered, "No, I am afraid."

Then Witch Boy went away and told the other to wait for him. So he left the poor boy there, and the poor little boy waited four days. He had nothing to eat, and he cried a great deal.

Eagle lived a little way to the north, and while he was in his nest he thought he heard something crying.

Next morning Eagle went out to hunt. About noon he remembered he had heard something crying in the night, and he said, "O dear, I wanted to go and see who was there to the south. I heard something crying just a like a human person. I wonder who it is, because no one ever comes up here."

Then Eagle went to the south and flew around four times. Finally he saw the little boy sitting in the crack in the rocks, fast asleep. Eagle came down and sat beside him. He was sitting there in his feathers, waiting. He thought the boy would never wake up.

Then he took off his feather dress and turned into a human person. He went over to the boy and touched him over the heart; then he awoke.

"My child, whoever you are, wake up," he said, "I am here. You were left alone and I have come." Then the little boy woke up. But he was so miserable that he just opened his eyes a little and shut them again.

Then Eagle Man said, "Please, little boy, wake up. I shall carry you on my back and take you to your home."

The little boy opened his eyes when he heard that Eagle Man would carry him home. Then he said, "Yes, please. I am hungry and thirsty, and I am not strong enough to go home alone. Please take me."

Then Eagle took him and tried to make him stand up, but the boy was so weak he fell right down.

Then Eagle said, "Now, you try to open your eyes and I shall carry you on my back. You hold onto me and I shall take you down."

So Eagle left the boy and went off a little way to put on his feather dress. When he came back, the boy grasped him by the neck.

"Now, shut your eyes and we shall go down to your home," said Eagle.

The people were living at K'iakima. It was in the afternoon, when the sun turns over, that Eagle took him down. The little boy was the son of a Kachina chief, and the people had been looking everywhere for him for four days. The mother and father of the little boy were crying all the time. This was the last day the people were going to look for him; then they would have to give him up as lost.

Just as they were coming home, Eagle brought the boy down to the spring to give him a drink. He set him down, and said, "Now, open your eyes." The little boy dropped down, for his heart was weak. They sat down beside the spring, and Eagle said, "Now, drink. Then you will feel better and you will walk home. Your home is right there, just a little way off. Please hurry! I am afraid someone will come and find out that I brought you down!"

While little boy was drinking, Eagle plucked out six of his tail feathers, and he took downy feathers from under his wings, and from his shoulders he took the "spoon feathers." Then he pulled up some grass that was growing by the spring and tied it around the feathers.

He then said to the boy: "Now, you have had a drink, so walk home and take these along to your father. Your parents know that you went with that Witch Boy to look for birds' nests. Take these feathers to your father. Do not tell him that I gave them to you, but tell him that I brought you down. Your father will know what to do with the feathers." Then Eagle flew to his home.

The little boy started for home, walking weakly as if he would fall down at each step.

The women were coming to get water at the spring. When they saw the little boy coming, one of them set down her jar and ran up to him and cried: "O my son! We know that you have been lost, and all the people have been looking for you. Where have you been?"

"Up in the mountains," said the little boy.

"What have you there?" asked the woman.

"I have only feathers. Do not touch them!" cried the little boy. The woman kept saying, "I would like to feel them."

The boy did not want her to touch the feathers; but she did, and right away she turned into an owl and went off screeching.

Now she lives near a spring right below where Eagle lives, because she touched the eagle feathers, which had magical power.

Then the little boy said to himself, "Now, if anyone else meets me I will not let him touch my feathers." So he went home. Everyone saw him coming with the eagle feathers and ran in to tell his mother and father.

They could hardly believe it was their little boy, so changed was he. They came out just as the boy was struggling to climb the ladder. He was so weak he could not climb, so his father went down and brought him up on his back, the little boy still holding to his feathers.

When he came in, the boy said, "Mother, put down a basket." She brought a basket and he laid the feathers in it.

Then he said: "Father, I brought you these feathers. Eagle brought me down and left me at the spring. I walked home. These are eagle feathers."

The father took the feathers and breathed in from them and said, "Father of Eagles, give me long life and your strong heart. You travel so far and fly so high that your breath is clear and powerful. Make my heart clean like yours. I breathe from your feathers, so make me strong like you."

Then he thanked Eagle because he had brought his boy back.

Right away the father knew what to do with the feathers. He said, "Our fathers, the Kachinas, will wear these feathers because Eagle is strong and wise and kind. He travels far in all directions, so he will surely bring us the rains. The eagle feathers must always come first."

That is why the Kachinas always wear eagle feathers, because Eagle found the little boy and brought him down and sent his feathers with him. They always pray to him for good health because Eagle flies high where the air is clean. He never goes where there is dirt and sickness. ❖

HOW BEES LEARNED TO FLY AND
HOW PEACHES BECAME SWEETER

MOMO (BEE) KACHINA

Bee Woman and Asya Bird Woman lived in neighboring villages. They were very good friends, and both had children. The Bird Woman liked to walk around in the peach orchard north of her house and eat peaches, which she liked very much.

One day Bird Woman went to the neighboring village to visit her friend Bee Woman. They talked all day long about their children and their gardens and many things. Then Bee Woman gave Bird Woman some honey to eat, which she enjoyed very much.

In the evening Asya Bird Woman returned to her own home, after inviting Bee Woman to come and spend the next day with her. Bee Woman said she would be glad to do so.

The next morning Bee Woman started early to go to her friend's house, for at that time bees had no wings, and walked very slowly.

Asya Bird Woman lived in an opening in a rock, which the Bee entered. The Asya invited Bee Woman to have a seat, and then offered her some peaches. "Do you like these peaches?" Asya Woman asked.

"Yes," answered Bee Woman, "I always eat them. I like them very much. I live on them. But," said she, "these are not good, they are sour.

What do you think, shall I make some medicine for them so that they will taste sweeter?" (For, you know, peaches were not sweet then as they are now.)

"Very well," Bird Woman replied, "make some medicine then, and I shall have something that tastes good."

So Bee Woman put some honey on the peaches, and ever since then the peaches are sweet and taste better. Bird Woman was very happy, and said to Bee Woman, "I am glad, and I shall give you something, too, because you have made my peaches taste better."

Bird Woman pulled out some of her feathers, made some wings, and attached them to the Bee, saying to her, "Now, fly!"

But Bee Woman answered, "I do not know how it is done."

"You just extend your front legs," said Bird Woman.

Bee Woman did as she was told. She moved her front legs and flew away.

Ever since that visit, peaches have been sweet and bees can fly. ❖

How the Deer
Got Their Red Eyes

KWEYWUH
(WOLF)
KACHINA

Old Deer Woman and Old Wolf Woman were good friends. They used to go out together after wood and food. One day when they were out gathering wood, both became tired, so they sat down to rest under a juniper tree. Wolf Woman asked Deer Woman to let her comb her hair. When Deer Woman sat down, Wolf Woman hit her and killed her. Then Wolf Woman got some meat and took it home to her children. When she was passing the house of Deer Woman's children, she gave them a piece of meat and told them their mother would be late coming home that night. Then the little Deer Children took the piece of meat inside to roast it.

As the children were roasting the meat, it started to talk. The meat said it was their mother's flesh and that Old Wolf Woman had killed her. So the children sat down and cried all night long.

Next morning Wolf Woman went out to the mountain to get the rest of her meat. The little Wolf Children and the little Deer Children came out to play together. The Wolf Children asked the Deer Children how they got such pretty red eyes.

The Deer Children told the Wolf Children that if they wished to have pretty eyes too, they would show them how to get them. So they took a lot of corn-cobs, started a fire, and shut the Wolf Children inside the cave. Then the Deer Children ran away before Old Wolf Woman came back.

When the Wolf Woman returned, she found her two children smothered to death, so she ran after the Deer Children.

The Deer Children ran until they came to a flock of Blackbirds, which they asked to help them escape from Wolf Woman. So the Blackbirds put the children inside of a football and kicked the football down south.

By and by the Wolf Woman came to the Blackbirds and asked them if they had seen the Deer Children run by. The Blackbirds did not answer. Soon the Deer Children came to a river, where they told Beaver to take them across. When Wolf Woman came there, she asked Beaver to take her across.

After the old Wolf Woman got on Beaver's back, he began to dive, and it took a long time to cross the river. By that time the Deer Children had reached the cave where the other Deer were living, and they told the Deer what had happened to their mother.

Then all the male Deer began to sharpen their horns to wait for Wolf Woman. Soon she came. The Deer told her to pass in. The Deer Children were in there. As soon as Wolf Woman came down, the old male Deer caught her on their horns and killed her, and they made soup out of her.

All the Deer were told not to drop any soup on the floor, for it they did so, some Wolf would come out from the den. One of the Deer Children happened to drop some soup on the floor. Whereupon a lot of Wolves came running, and ever since that time wolves and deer have been enemies, and the deer have red eyes because the little Deer Children cried so hard when Old Wolf Woman killed their mother, Old Deer Woman. ❖

The Foster Child of the Deer

TAWA
(SUN)
KACHINA

Once, long, long ago, at the old Zuni village of Hawikuh, there lived a very beautiful maiden. Her father was a great priest and had devoted her to sacred things. Therefore, he always kept her in the house, secure from the gaze of all men, and thus she grew.

The maiden was so beautiful that, when the Sun looked down along one of the straight beams of his own light as it passed through the sky-hole of the house, he beheld her and wondered at her rare beauty, unable to compare it with anything he saw in his great journeys around the world.

As the maiden grew into a young woman, the Sun loved her exceedingly and finally descended to earth on one of his own beams of light, entering her room. Suddenly, while she was sitting one noonday weaving a pretty basket, there stood before her a handsome youth, beautifully dressed. He looked upon her gently and lovingly, and she was not afraid, for it was the Sun Father himself. So it came about that the maiden loved him and he loved her, and he won her to be his wife. He always came to visit her at noon-time, when his sunbeam came into her room.

Now the young wife was to become a mother, and as no one knew that she was married to the Sun Father, she decided to hide the child when he was born. So when the time came, she carefully wrapped the baby in soft cotton, and in the middle of the night she stole out over the housetops and laid him in a sheltered place near the little stream in the valley. Then, weeping, she went back to her room.

As daylight was breaking, a Deer with her two little speckled fawns descended from the hills to the valley, and stopped at the stream to drink. Suddenly they heard an infant's cry, and looking up they saw dust and cotton and other things flying about in the air, like a little whirlwind blowing. It was the little baby kicking, hungry, alone and cold.

"Bless my delight!" cried the Deer. "I have this day found a deserted child, and though it be human, it shall be mine. I love you so much, my children, that sure I can love another." She, therefore, breathed her warm breath upon the child and caressed it until it became quiet. Then she wrapped it again in cotton and gently lifting it on to her broad horns, carried it away to the south. Her children ran beside her, crying, "Ney! Ney!" in their delight. They went to their nice warm home in the clump of pinon and juniper trees.

The Deer was delighted next morning to find that the boy had grown greatly. She had given it some milk, and by the time the sun went down, the baby was already creeping about. Great was her surprise to find that this baby grew even more swiftly than the deer! One evening of the fourth day it was running around, playing with its foster brother and sister. He was also swift of foot, even as compared with those little deer.

Behold! On the eighth day it was youth fair to look upon. He wondered why he was not clothed like his foster brother and sister, in soft warm hair, with pretty spots on it.

He grew wondrously strong as he ran about, and even swifter of foot than the Deer themselves. He learned the language of the Deer and all their ways. When he had learned all that a deer should know, the Deer Mother led him forth into the wilds and made him acquainted with the great herd to which she belonged.

The herd of Deer were exceedingly happy to have the youth, and loved him so much that they soon made him the leader of the Deer in the Hawikuh country. When they were out on the mesas, running to and fro, the swift youth ran at their head and led them. The soles of his feet became hard as the hooves of the Deer, the skin of his person strong and dark, the hair on his head long and soft and waving.

Now, it chanced one morning, late that summer, that the maiden's uncle went out hunting. He took his way past the lair of the Deer Mother and her foster child. Looking beyond the mesas, he saw a great herd of Deer as if in council. They were quiet, and seemed to be listening intently to someone in their midst. The hunter stole carefully on hands and knees, crawling among the bushes until he came nearer. What was his wonder to behold a splendid youth, broad of shoulder, tall and strong of limb, sitting on the ground, and all the Deer, old and young, paying attention to what he was saying.

The hunter rubbed his eyes again and again, and finally raised himself up to peer yet more closely, when the sharp eyes of the youth discovered him. With a shout he raised himself up on his feet and sped away, the whole herd of Deer following him with a thundering of hooves.

The hunter dropped his bow and ran home as fast as he could and told the maiden's father what he had seen. The old priest summoned his hunters and warriors, and had the uncle repeat the story. "Alas, alas! You have seen a spirit which will bring evil to your family!" said they. But he convinced them it was a mortal youth, so they decided to form a grand hunt. On the fourth day the people would gather in from all sides, and surround the herd, and possibly capture or at least see this youth.

Now, when the Deer had gone to a safe distance, they ran more slowly and called to their leader not to fear. Then the old Foster Mother told them how she had found him and that he was human.

The youth sat thinking deeply. Then he raised his head proudly, and said: "Even though I be the child of mortals, they have not loved me; they have cast me from their midst, therefore will I be faithful to you."

But the Deer Mother said to him: "Hush, my child, you are but a human, and though you might live on the roots of trees and bushes and plants in summer and autumn, in winter you can not live, for the fruits and nuts will all be gone." All of the old members of the herd told him the same thing. They also said that on the fourth day they would be hunted, as was the custom when they had been seen by man.

A splendid Deer rose and came forward, laid his cheek on the cheek of the boy, and said, "Yet we love you, but we must now part from you. Come now with me to the Land of the Souls (Sacred Lake), so that you may be like other humans, only exceeding them."

The youth was finally convinced, and together they set out. As the Deer neared the shore of the lake, he said: "Step in boldly with me. Ladders of rushes will rise to receive you, and down underneath the waters into the great Halls of the Dead we will be borne gently and swiftly." They stepped into the Lake. Brighter and lighter it grew, and they were borne downward into halls of splendor, lighted by many lights and fires. A large number of the gods were sitting in council silently. Pautiwa (Pah-oo-tee-wah), the Sun Priest of the Sacred Drama, Shulawitsi (Shoo-lah-weet-see), the God of Fire, with his torch of ever-living flame, and many others were there.

When the strangers arrived, they greeted and were greeted. Sacred dancers came in from all directions and performed to the delight of the gods and the wonder of the Deer and his foster brother.

Then Pautiwa arose and said, "What would you have, O Deer of the forest mesas, with your companion; for not thinking of nothing would one visit the home of the gods."

Then the Deer lifted his head and told his story.

"It is well," said the gods.

The gods made the youth acquainted with the speech of mortal man. Then they called out and there were brought before them and given to the youth fine garments of white cotton embroidered in many colors, rare necklaces of sacred shell, with many turquoises and coral-like stones, and all that the most beautifully clad of our ancient people could have wished for.

Pautiwa said at parting: "Fear not! Happy will you be in the days to come. Return with the Deer and do as you are told."

Then the Deer led the Sun youth out with his bundle, to go back to his last meeting place with his friends, the Deer.

On the morning when the hunters of Hawikuh were setting forth, the Deer gathered themselves in a vast herd on the southern mesa, and they circled about the Sun youth and instructed him how to untie the bundle he had brought. They ran swiftly around him, and breathed fierce, moist breath, until hot steam covered him from head to foot. Then the youth put on the costume, as he had seen the dancers do at the Sacred Lake. Into his hair at the back, under the band which he placed around the temples, he thrust bright feathers of the macaw.

A great many Deer volunteered to die for the youth. Soon there was an alarm! The Deer began to scatter, and then to assemble and scatter again. At last the hunters, with drawn bows, came running in, and soon their arrows were flying in the midst of those who were devoted, and Deer after Deer fell, pierced to their hearts.

At last only a few were left, amongst them the Deer Mother and

her two children. Taking the lead, the glorious youth, although bur-
dened by his new dress, sped forth with them. They ran and ran, the
fleetest of the hunters chasing them. Finally only the uncle and his brave
sons were in pursuit. The Deer foster brother was slain, and then his
Deer foster sister. The youth was angry, but remembering his instruc-
tions, ran on. At last only he and his old Deer Mother were left. Then
the hunters caught the Deer Mother, but they did not kill her because
she had cared for the youth. They merely turned her away, then renewed
the chase. The youth now turned and faced them like a stag at bay, and
said, "O, my uncle, what would you do?"

The uncle wondered who the youth was, and why he called him
uncle. So the youth told him what the Deer Mother had told him about
being picked up as an infant, and what good care the Deer Mother had
given him. The uncle decided there was a likeness to the boy's mother,
so they sent messengers ahead to find out. It was all true, and the priest
father scolded the maiden for leaving her child. She cried to have him
brought back, thinking he was still a baby.

When the hunters came back with the handsome youth in their
midst, he went to his mother, who threw her arms around him and
wept. But he said, "O, mother, do not weep, for I have come to you and
I will cherish you." And so was the foster-child of the Deer restored to
his mother and his people.

Wondrously wise in the ways of the Deer and their language was
he — so much so that, seeing them, he understood them. This youth
made little ado of hunting, for he knew that he could pay those rites
and attentions to the Deer that were most acceptable, and made them
glad of death at the hand of the hunter. And ere long, so great was his
knowledge and success, and his preciousness in the eyes of the Master
of Life, that by his will and his arm alone the people of Hawikuh were
fed and were clad in buckskins.

A rare and beautiful maiden the foster child married, and most
happy was he with her. So he and his people became the greatest
people in Hawikuh.

Now the sorcerers of that tribe became envious of his prosperity,
and sought to diminish it in many ways, wherein they failed.

At last one night the Master of Sorcerers in secret places raised his
voice and cried: "Weh-h-h-h! Weh-h-h-h!" And round about him presently gathered all the sorcerers of the place, and they entered into a deep
cavern, large and lighted by green, glowing fires, and there, staring at

one another, they devised means to destroy this splendid youth, the child of the Sun.

One of their number stood forth and said: "I will destroy him in his own vocation. He is a hunter, and the Coyote loves well to follow the hunter." His words were received with acclamation, and the youth who had offered himself sped forth in the night to prepare, by incantation and with his infernal appliances, a disguise for himself.

On the next morning, when the youth went forth to hunt, an old Coyote sneaked behind him after he reached the mesas, and, following stealthily, waited his throwing down of the Deer; and when the youth had called and killed a number of Deer and sat down to rest on a fallen tree, the Coyote sneaked into sight. The youth, looking at him, merely thought: "He seeks the blood of my slain Deer," and he went on with his prayers and sacrifices to the dead of the Deer. But soon, stiffening his limbs, the Coyote swiftly scudded across the open, and with a puff from his mouth and nostrils like a sneeze toward the youth, threw himself against him and arose a man — the same man who had offered his services in the council of the wizards — while the poor youth, falling over, ran away, a human being still, in heart and mind, but in form a coyote.

Off to the southward he wandered, his tail dragging in the dust. Growing hungry, he had naught to eat; and, cold, on the sides of the mesas, he passed the night. On the following morning he wandered still, until at last, very hungry, he even nipped the blades of grass and ate the berries of the juniper. Thus he became ill and worn; and one night as he was seeking a warm place to lie down and die, he saw a little red light glowing from the top of a hillock. Toward this light he took his way, and when he came near he saw that it was shining up through the sky-hole of someone's house. He peered over the edge and saw an old Badger with his grizzly wife, sitting before a fire, not in the form of a badger but in the form of a little man, his badger-skin hanging beside him.

Then the youth said to himself: "I will cast myself down into their house, thus showing them my miserable condition." And as he tried to step down the ladder, he fell on the floor before them.

The Badgers were disgusted. They grabbed the Coyote, and hauling him up the ladder, threw him into the plain, where he fell far away and swooned from loss of breath. When he recovered his thoughts he again turned toward the glowing sky-hole, and crawling feebly back, threw himself down into the room again. Again he was thrown out, but this time the Badger said, "It is marvelously strange that this Coyote, the miserable fellow, should insist on coming back, and coming back."

"I have heard," said the little old Badger-woman, "that our glorious beloved youth of Hawikuh was changed some time ago into a Coyote. It may be he. Let us see when he comes again if it be he. For the love of mercy, let us see!"

Ere long the youth again tried to clamber down the ladder, and fell with a thud on the floor before them. A long time he lay there senseless, but at last opened his eyes and looked about. The Badgers eagerly asked if he were the same who had been changed into a Coyote, or condemned to inhabit the form of one. The youth could only move his head in acquiescence.

Then the Badgers hastily gathered an emetic and set it to boil, and when ready they poured the fluid down the throat of the seeming Coyote, and tenderly held him and pitied him. Then they laid him before the fire to warm him. The old Badger, looking about in some of his burrows, found a sacred crystal, and heating it to glowing heat in the fire, he seared the palms of the youth's hands, the soles of his feet, and the crown of his head, repeating incantations as he performed this last operation, whereupon the skin burst and fell off, and the youth, haggard and lean, lay before them. They nourished him as best they could, and, when well recovered, sent him home to join his people again and render them happy. Clad in his own fine garments, happy of countenance and handsome as before, and, according to his regular custom, bearing a deer on his back, returned the youth to his people, and there he lived most happily.

As I have said, this was in the days of the ancients, and it is because this youth lived so long with the Deer and became acquainted with this every way and their every word, and taught all that he knew to his children and to others whom he took into his friendship, that we have today a class of men — the Sacred Hunters of our tribe — who surpassingly understand the ways and the language of the Deer. ❖

TIHKUYI CREATES THE GAME ANIMALS

NUVA
(SNOW)
KACHINA

A party of Hopi boys were trapping mice, which were the only meat the first Hopi people had. The mouse-trap was a flat stone propped up by a short, slanting stick. The base of the stick rested on a grain of corn. When a mouse gnawed at the corn, the stick moved and the stone fell on the mouse.

At night, after the traps were set, the boys roasted some ears of corn which they had brought from home. The leader of the hunt said that they would burn the cobs, and while doing so they would call upon someone and see if any one would come. So the cobs were put into the fire, and in a little while a wailing voice was heard.

The chief of the hunt said, "Listen! Somebody is coming!" He filled a little smoking pipe which his father had given him, and handed it about the circle of boys. All smoked. Then the chief ordered more wood put on the fire. A larger fire was built up, and in a short time a fairy woman came in from the darkness.

Now the boys were frightened and drew close together. The chief, however, said: "Do not be afraid of her. I think she is our fairy mother." It was Tikhkuyi (Tee-Koo-yee).

The fairy woman spoke: "Little boys, do not fear me. You have called me by throwing corn-cobs into the fire, and I have come to help you. You are here catching mice. But mice are too small for meat. I am going to sing and see if we can bring larger game."

The fairy woman began to sing. After she had finished, she said: "Try to remember that song, and when you go home, tell your sisters to sing it while they are grinding corn. If the Chiefs of the Four Directions have heard our song, we shall know it tomorrow. When you get up in the morning and look about for larger game, look for this." On the ground the fairy woman made marks like rabbit-tracks. "So follow these marks if you see them, and pull the animals out of the rocks," she said. Then she went away after the boy chief had given her a prayer-stick, on which feathers were fastened, as a gift for her kindness.

Before the boys went to bed, snow began to fall. In the morning the snow was up to the ankles. When the boys got up, they were surprised to see the ground all covered with white, for they had never before seen snow. They made moccasins of rags and the bits of blankets in which they had carried food from their homes. Then they took sticks and went out to hunt. A little way from camp they found rabbit-tracks, and each boy followed a trail as the fairy mother had instructed them. Many rabbits were dragged from their holes among the rocks. When the boys returned, they waited for Tihkuyi to come and instruct them.

After the evening meal, the boys roasted corn and threw the cobs into the fire. Tihkuyi again appeared, and said, "Those are cottontail rabbits, and this is the way to dress them." She showed them how to skin a rabbit and how to clean it, and then told them to dry the skins and take them home so that their mothers might make rabbit-fur robes. "Since you have me for your mother," she said, "let one of you call your father." Then the boy chief stepped aside and called, "If there is anybody about here who is our fairy father, let him come!"

In a little while they heard a voice in a long-drawn wail, but in a lower tone than the voice of Tihkuyi. Footsteps were heard, and the chief ordered a larger fire built. When the new-comer approached, the boys were greatly frightened, but their chief was calm, and said to the man, "Come, our fairy father, and sit down." They then saw that it was Masou (Mah-so-oo).

Then Tihkuyi said, "You have the rabbits, but tomorrow there will be more snow, and you will go out into the valley and see if you cannot find still larger game."

Both Tihkuyi and Masou marked on the ground the tracks of a jack-rabbit. Masou said: "When you go home, try hunting the jack-rabbits in the valley near your village. But if you want still larger game, go into another valley below the knoll called Huk-yat-vi." Then the boy chief gave a prayer-stick to Masou, who at once disappeared with Tihkuyi.

The next morning there was twice as much snow as before, and the boys had to tear up some of their blankets to make leggings. In the valley they found tracks of jack-rabbits, and trailing the animals to the bushes where they were hiding, they killed many, striking them on the head with their sticks. The following morning they started home, piling the meat on frames made by lashing two sticks parallel, and covering them with the skins. When they were nearing home, they built a fire, and the fathers of the boys started out to meet them. From a distance they saw that the children had something larger than mice, and quickly sent a runner back with word that all the fathers should come down and carry the loads home.

The men were eager to hunt where the boys had hunted, but the boy chief said: "Just wait. We will try here."

"There are none here," the men said.

But the boy chief insisted that they should try hunting near the village. A few days later he told the village chief that on the following day they would have a rabbit-hunt. The chief agreed, and everybody was told about it.

When the hunt began, some of the young men who had joined the party without really expecting to find game so close to the village, expressed their doubt; but when the circle of hunters had been formed and the men gradually came together, many rabbits were rounded up and killed. From that time rabbits have lived in the valley. They were the children of Tihkuyi.

One day the boy chief told the village chief that they would look for larger game in the direction of Huk-yat-vi. He asked that everybody be told that the next day they would go to that place for rats and mice, but the men should carry heavier clubs than their rabbit sticks. So the next day the hunters went forth, and on the south side of Huk-yat-vi they formed into a circle which they gradually drew in smaller and smaller. The boy chief went inside the circle of men and there Masou was surrounded by deer and antelope. Immediately Masou disappeared, and called to the boy chief to shout.

When the boy chief shouted, the antelope and the deer were frightened and ran round and round in the circle. He told the men to draw together at the places where the animals were trying to break through. When the antelope and deer were becoming weary, the men drew in toward the center, and when the animals finally fell down, the men rushed in and struck them with clubs. All came home heavily laden with meat and skins. From that time the people lived on the flesh of rabbits, deer, and antelope. ❖

THE K'YAKLU BEING
AND THE DUCK

PAWIK
(DUCK)
KACHINA

Whan the world was still new, the Shi-wi-na-kwe (Zuni people) were searching for the middle of the world where there would be a warm climate and the earth would not quake. For now the earth was always rumbling and quaking, and the people, in great fear, went ever on in search of the middle, where they could build homes and raise corn, and be happy.

Now, they had always traveled all together, but as the number of people had increased greatly, traveling became difficult, so they decided to send messengers in different directions to find signs of the middle.

There was a priest of the people named K'ya-kwi-mo-si, who had a son named K'yaklu. Now K'yaklu was wiser of words and understanding than all others, having listened to the councils of men with all beings, since the beginning of the new-made world. So K'yaklu was summoned and told that he was chosen to seek the middle of the world by going toward the northland. He said, "Yes, as my father and the great ones wish." So he started out.

K'yaklu wandered far to the north, where he found all the land covered with snow and ice, and was dazzlingly white. He became bitterly cold—so cold that his face became white from his frozen breath, and white like all creatures who live there.

Now, K'yaklu could not find his way out, and he was lost. He became so cold at night and dreary of heart, so lost by day and blinded by light, that he continually wept and cried aloud, until the tears running down his cheeks made deep furrows. His lips became cracked with continual calling, and his voice grew shrill and dry-sounding like the voices of far-flying waterfowl. As he cried, wandering blindly here and there, these water-birds, hearing, flocked around him in great numbers, calling to one another.

Behold! When K'yaklu heard the waterfowl calling, their meanings were plain to him, for he could understand their language. Yet still he lamented, because none of them told him the way back to his country and people.

Now, when the Duck heard K'yaklu's cry, she came closer, answering loudly. As K'yaklu was the listener and speaker, and wisest of all men, so Duck was the traveler and searcher, knowing all ways, whether above or below the waters, whether in the north, west, south, or east, and so the most knowing of all creatures.

So K'yaklu, in the midst of his lamentations, sought counsel of Duck, telling her: "Here am I, searching for the middle of the world for my people, lost and blind in this land of whiteness. When the Sun rises and passes, all things are so bright that my eyes see only darkness; and in the darkness all ways are bewildered! I hear the voice of the Winds, but they speak of all regions, and none tell me the way to the middle! Ha-na-ha! Ha-na-ha! A-hah-hua!"

"Hold, my father," said Duck. "Think no longer sad thoughts. Though you are blind, yet you hear all, as I see all. Give me tinkling shells from your girdle and place them on my neck and in my beak. Thus will I guide you, if you will grasp and hold firmly my tail, for I know the way well, going that way every year leading Wild Geese and Cranes to a warm climate."

And so K'yaklu placed his talking shells on Duck's neck, and in her beak he placed the singing shells, which in his speakings and listenings K'yaklu had always worn at his girdle; and, though painfully and lamely, he followed the sound made by the shells, perching lightly on his search-

ing outstretched hand, and did all too slowly follow her swift flight
from place to place, and she would dip her head, making the shells call
loudly.

By and by they came to the country of thick mists and rains on the
border of the Snow World, and passed from water to water, until at last,
wider waters lay in the way. In vain Duck called and jingled her shells
from over the midst of them; K'yaklu could not follow. All crippled
was he; nor could he swim or fly as could Duck.

Now, Rainbow Worm was near, and when he heard the sacred
sounds of the shells, he listened. "Ha!" said he, "these are my grandchildren, and precious are they, for they call one to the other with shells
of the great world-encircling waters." And with one measure of his length,
he arched his way to them.

"Why do you mourn, my grandchildren? Give your plume-sticks to
me, and I shall bear you swiftly on my shoulders to your people and
country." So K'yaklu took his lightest and choicest plume-sticks, and
Duck gave to him her two strong wing-feathers. Rainbow Worm arched
himself and stooped near, while K'yaklu, breathing on the plumes,
approached him and fastened them to his heart side.

"Thanks this day!" said Rainbow Worm. "Mount, now, on my shoulders, grandson!" Rainbow Worm unbent himself lower that K'yaklu
might mount. Then he arched himself high amidst the clouds, bearing
K'yaklu upward in one swoop, while Duck spread her wings in flight
toward the south. Like an arrow, Rainbow Worm straightened himself
forward and followed until his face looked into the Lake of the Ancients.

And there in the plain to the north of the Sacred Lake, K'yaklu
descended from the back of Rainbow Worm, who stretched himself
and went quickly back whence he had come.

But, alas! K'yaklu was weary and lame. He could not journey farther,
but sat himself down to rest and to think of the way.

Then again Duck spread her wings and flew to the Sacred Lake.
There she swam to and fro, up and down, loudly quacking and calling.
Lo! The lights of the ceremonial room of the Dance of Good began to
gleam in the waters, and as she gazed, Duck beheld, rising from them,
snout foremost, like one of her own kind, the Salamopia of the north,
whom the gods had sent to bid Duck dive down and lay before them
whatever message she might bear. Duck followed down, down, into
the great assembly halls. There she told of the far journeys she had
made, of her finding and leading K'yaklu, and how now K'yaklu sat

blind, lame, and deaf in the plain beyond the mountains.

"Yes, we know him well!" replied the gods, "And because of the hardships he has endured, we wish to help him." So the gods instructed Duck to go upward, and tinkle her shells, thereby summoning the House Priests, the children of the mountains, and instruct them to make a litter of poles and reeds and bear K'yaklu to the Sacred Lake and down to the home of the gods, and they would tell him many things.

So Duck did as she was told, and the House Priests made the litter, and, singing, went to the plain where K'yaklu was sitting. They lifted him to their shoulders, and, singing loudly, they lightly bore him to the shores of the deep black lake, where gleamed from the middle the lights of the gods.

Salamopia again rose to the top, and his assistants took K'yaklu on their shoulders and bore him over the water to the magic ladder of rushes and canes which reared itself high out of the water. And K'yaklu, scattering prayer-meal before him, stepped down the way, slowly, like a blind man, descending a sky-hole. No sooner had he taken four steps than the ladder lowered into the deep; and lo! his light was instantly darkened.

But when they entered the assembly hall of the gods, Little Fire God lifted his fire-brand on high, and, swinging it, lighted the fires anew, so that K'yaklu saw again with his full sight, and he saw all the gods assembled. And he saw Pa-u-ti-wa and his warriors, the Blue Horns, the tall Shalako People, and all the god-priests of the six regions. And Pautiwa greeted him, saying: "Sit down with us, that of much we may tell you, for you have wandered far and changed much. You are cherished among us for keeping unbroken the Tale of Creation, and we shall tell you of past and future days."

Then K'yaklu sat down and bowed his head, and called to Duck, who has guided him. Duck came and perched upon K'yaklu's outstretched hand. The gods sent forth their runners to summon all beings, and gathered themselves in a sacred song-circle, called in dancers from the several chambers and they danced the Dance of Good. And with them came the little ones who had sunk beneath the waters while their mothers were carrying them across the muddy river and had died. And here they were all well and happy, and clothed in white cotton mantles and precious neck jewels. And these little children played, only sad with the sadness of their mothers who mourned them as lost.

When the dancers stopped, the gods told K'yaklu all the things he should know and tell to his people. Then they brought forth a sacred pipe, and after all had smoked, the Salamopia lifted the ladder and guided K'yaklu and Duck safely up to the shore of the lake.

The sacred clowns (Ko-ye-ma-shi) heard the tinkling of the shells and came forth with their litter. Then K'yaklu told them that from now the gods had willed that they give enjoyment to men, and comfort them in their sorrows. Then he bade them carry him to his people. So with much singing and fun-making the ten sacred clowns conducted K'yaklu to his people. They made so much fun all the way, that all the people ran out to see who was coming. No one was frightened, but thought how good-natured they were, and like them. They knew it was some one important, because he was being guided by the far-journeying Duck.

And so they came to the village of their people, and with much rejoicing the people greeted the long-lost K'yaklu, and gave him food and drink, and gave clothes to the sacred clowns which they wore in a disorderly way to make people laugh.

Then they all gathered in secret council, and holding Duck in his hand, K'yaklu spoke to the sound of the shell, and told the tales of creation which the gods had told him, and of his wanderings, and they were happy to have him back again. ❖

THE RETURN OF THE CORN MAIDS

PAUTIWA
KACHINA

Long ago the Zuni people were starving. The Corn Maids had run away because the people were careless about the corn. So the Corn Maids ran away and went to the village of the masked gods, or Kachinas.

The people played with corn-bread and threw it away, and they threw the corn carelessly into the corn rooms. They did not pile it up neatly the way we do now.

So Yellow Corn Maid went to all the houses in the night and told the Corn Maids to come with her. They said, "All right, we shall go."

Now, they did not know where to go. Pautiwa (Pah-oo-tee-wah) in the village of the Kachinas heard them, and he said to Yellow Corn Maid: "I have heard that you have decided to run away and that you do not know where to go. I do not want you to go away. Come with me so that my people will not always be punished. They will learn again." Pautiwa did not want them to go away to some other people. So he said, "Come with me, I will hide you."

So all the Corn Maids, Yellow, Blue, Red, White, Speckled and Black, followed him. Black Corn Maid went behind to make the road dark so that the people would not find them.

Pautiwa took them with him and lay them all down in the middle of the Sacred Lake, and said: "Now, my children, be very still and do not talk, as I do not want anyone below to know that you are here." So Pautiwa stayed outside in the middle of the lake, and when the people came out to ask him whatever they wanted to know, they never noticed that he was hiding the Corn Maids.

Now, at Itiwana, the Middle Place, the people had plenty of corn, but it was not good. There was not meat on it. All the corn piled in the rooms looked sick. They planted the seeds, but nothing came up. The heart of the corn had gone to the village of the Kachinas.

One year passed and the next came, and the people had nothing. In some houses where they had looked after their corn right, they still had some. Finally the careless people went to work for the other people. They wove and spun, and ground corn for them, so they could get something to eat. Finally they gave away everything they had in exchange for a basket of corn. So they were punished.

Now, the priests knew that the Corn Maids had gone off, but they did not know what to do to get them back, nor did they know where they had fled. So they held a council of all the head men. They decided to send the Medicine Flower Boys, who are very wise, in search of the Corn Maids. So they went all over, to all the lakes and to the ocean. They looked in all directions, but they could not find them.

Then they called Jimson Weed Boy. He went in all directions, but could not find them. Then the War Gods tried. They sent down a Fly into the west, just a little dirty House Fly. In the village of the Kachinas they knew that the Corn Maids were hiding. All the Kachina women were inside cooking by the fire, and the Kachina children were playing outside. The children ran inside, and said, "Fly is coming!" The Kachina women were wise. They knew that the War Gods had sent Fly to find the Corn Maids, so they said to the little Kachinas, "Here, take this pumpkin stew and set it down outside so that Fly will go for it and burn her tongue." And so they did. Fly came along and went right for the stew because it was sweet. She burned her tongue. That is why the fly has never been able to talk since then and could not tell the War Gods where the Corn Maids were hiding.

Then the War Gods sent Arrows up into the sky. The Arrows went all around, but did not see anything except the wind. So at last the War Gods went to the priests who were waiting in their ceremonial rooms, fasting and praying, and told them: "We are not so wise, our fathers, as the one who has hidden the Corn Maids. We have always been able to help you before, but now you will have to find someone wiser." So they said, for the War Gods had brought the people up from under the earth when the earth was new, and had been with them to help them ever since.

"Try Newekwe (Nay-way-kway)," said they. "We have heard that he is as wise as we are." So they called a Newekwe man, and he planted prayer-sticks so that Newekwe would come. Now, Newekwe always sits on the Milky Way and can see everything that happens on the earth. So he came after sunset and asked the priests why they had sent for him.

"We have been starving for four years," said the priests, "and we have tried three times to find the Corn Maids, but none of our children have been successful."

Then Newekwe said, "If you really want the Corn Maids to return, I will see what I can do; but you must not drink nor eat, and you will sit here for four years (he meant four days) until I return."

So they promised that no matter how hungry or thirsty they might be, they would sit there and wait for his return, for they really wanted the Corn Maids to come back.

So Newekwe said: "I am going now. Make your thoughts and your hearts clean that I may bring the Corn Maids." Then he took ashes from the fireplace and went out.

When he got outside, he threw up the ashes, and right away there was a Milky Way in the sky. It came down to him and he jumped on it and sat down. It took him to the south and around to the east. It takes a person twenty days to go to the South Ocean, but he was wise and went in one day to the south and came back. He went to the north and the east and the west. He went to the west last, and there he dropped down from the Milky Way. Then he said to the Milky Way: "I have made you to protect my people. You will stay in the sky so that every-one will see you and watch you."

Newekwe came down in the west and dropped into the Sacred Lake. There Pautiwa was hiding the Corn Maids. He just walked through the lake and never got wet. He came to Pautiwa and said: "How are you, my father? Are the Corn Maids here?" Then Pautiwa was glad that he had come. Now he could rest. Then he said to the Corn Maids: "Now we shall go back to the Middle Place. They want you. They will treat you well because they want you badly. They have nothing to eat. Let us go."

So then Newekwe went first and the Corn Maids followed him. Then Pautiwa got up and dipped his water gourd into the lake and followed them. "Now I shall go with you and take this sacred water so that when my people plant the corn, the rain will always come," he said.

That is why Newekwe always bring the Corn Maids after Shalako, and Pautiwa brings the water in his water gourd so that all may have good luck with summer rains. ❖

HOW THE CORN PESTS WERE TRAPPED

HONAU
(BEAR)
KACHINA

I n the days of the Ancients, long, long ago, there lived in our town, which was then called the Middle Ant Hill of the World, a proud and beautiful maiden, the daughter of one of the richest men among our people. She had every possession a Zuni maiden could wish—blankets and mantles, embroidered dresses and sashes, deerskins and moccasins, turquoise earrings and shell necklaces, bracelets so many you could not count them. She had her mother and father, brothers and sisters, all of whom she loved very much. Why, therefore, should she care for anything else?

Yet there was one thing that troubled her. She had large corn-fields, so large and so many that those who worked them for her could not look after them properly. For, just as soon as the ears of corn became full and sweet with milk, all sorts of animals would break into the fields and eat up all of the nice sweet corn. Now, how to remove this difficulty, the poor girl did not know.

O, yes, there was another thing which troubled the maiden very much. All of the young men in the valley of our Ancients were very much in love with her. And besides, not a few of them had an eye to all of her possessions, and thought her home not an uncomfortable place to live. (For, you know, the Indian young man goes to live at the home of his wife's parents.) So these young men never gave the maiden of her family any peace, but came constantly to woo her. Finally, she said: "Look you! If any one of you will go to my cornfields and destroy or scare away the animal pests that eat up my corn, him I will marry and cherish, for I shall respect his ability and ingenuity."

The young men tried and tried to get rid of the pests, but it was of no use. The maiden's fame spread far and wide, and many a young man tried, but none could succeed.

There was a young fellow who lived in one of the outer towns, the poorest of the poor among the Zunis. Not only that, but he was so ugly that no woman would ever look at him without laughing. His only good feature was a pair of bright, twinkling eyes.

This ugly young man decided to try his luck. He had no present to offer the girl, as is the custom, so he went just as he was. He was received politely, and the old folk noticed that the girl seemed rather to like him. The maiden placed a tray of bread before him and bade him eat. After he had eaten, the old father said, "Let us smoke together." So they smoked.

By and by the old father asked if he were not thinking of something in coming to the house of a stranger. And the young man replied, it was very true; he felt ashamed to say it, but he wished to be accepted as a suitor for his daughter.

The maiden said she was well satisfied, but took the ugly young man aside and told him the conditions of his becoming her accepted husband. He smiled and said he would do his best.

The next day the ugly young man went down into the young maiden's cornfields. He dug a great deep pit with a sharp stick and a bone shovel. Now, when he had dug it — very smooth at the sides and top it was — he went to the mountain and got some poles, which he placed across the hole. Over the poles he spread earth, and set up cornstalks just as though no hole had been dug there. Then he put some very tempting bait, plenty of it, over the center of the poles, which were so weak that nobody, however light of foot, could walk over them without breaking through.

Night came on, and all the pests—Coyotes, Bears, Badgers, Gophers — came down slowly from the mountain. Now, Coyote was swift of foot, and he was the first one to reach the field. Nosing around and keeping a sharp lookout for watchers, he saw those tempting morsels that lay over the hole.

"Ha!" said he, and he gave a leap. In he went — sticks, dirt, bait, and all — to the bottom of the hole! He picked himself up, and rubbed the sand out of his eyes, then began to jump and jump, but he could not get out. Then he set up a dreadful howl.

Coyote had just stopped for breath, when Bear came along. "What in the name of all the witches are you howling for?" said Bear.

Coyote swallowed his whimpers immediately, and in a careless manner cried out: "Broadfoot, lucky, lucky fellow! Did you hear me sing? I am the happiest fellow in the world!"

"How's that?" asked Bear.

"Why, by the merest accident I fell into this hole. And what do you suppose I found down here? Green corn, meat, sweet-stuff, and everything a corn-eater could wish for. The only thing I lack is someone to enjoy my meal with me. Jump in, friend, and fall to. We'll have a jolly good night of it!"

So Old Bear drew back and jumped in. Then Coyote laughed and laughed. "Now get out if you can," said he to Bear. "You and I are in a pretty mess. True, I fell in by accident, but I would give my teeth and eyes if I could get out again!"

Bear came very near eating him up, but Coyote whispered something in his ear. "Good!" yelled Bear. "Ha! ha! ha! Fine idea! Let us sing together!"

So they laughed and sang and feasted until they attracted almost every corn-pest in the fields to see what they were doing. "Keep away, my friends!" cried Coyote. "No such luck for you! We got here first! Our spoils!"

"Can't I come? Can't I come?" cried out one after another.

"Well, yes — no; O, well, come on!" And the animals rushed in so fast that very soon the pit was almost full of them, scrambling to get ahead of one another. Then Coyote laughed, scrambled around some more, screamed at the top of his voice, climbed up over Bear, scrambled through the others who were snarling and biting, and skipped over their backs, out of the hole, and ran away laughing.

Now, the next morning down to the corn-field came the ugly

young man. An awful racket was coming from the pit. Looking over
the edge, the ugly young man saw the pit half full of every kind of
creature that had ever meddled with the corn-fields of man. Some of
them were all tired out, others were still trying to get out, jumping and
crawling and falling.

"Good, good, my friends!" cried the young man. "You must be
cold; I'll warm you up a little." So he gathered a quantity of dry wood,
threw it into the pit, lighted it, and burned the rascals all up. But he
noticed that Coyote was not there.

So the ugly young man went back to the house of the maiden and
reported to her what he had done. She was so pleased that she hardly
knew what to say. Then with a twinkle in her eye, she said, "Are you
quite sure they are all there?"

"Why, they are all there except Coyote," answered the young man.
"But I must tell you the truth—somehow he got out, or didn't get in.
"Who cares for a Coyote!" said the girl. "I would much rather marry a
man with some ingenuity about him than have all the Coyotes in the
world to kill." Whereupon she accepted this ugly young man who
showed such ingenuity, preferring one with brains and no money, to a
handsome one with riches and no ingenuity. And so it is today. Pretty
girls marry men who are no so handsome; rich girls marry poor ones;
and rich young men marry poor girls.

Thus it was in the days of the Ancients. Coyote got out of the trap
set for him by the ugly young man. That is the reason why coyotes are
so much more abundant than any other corn-pests in the land of Zuni,
and do what you will, they are sure to get away with some of your
corn, anyhow. ❖

THE COCK AND THE MOUSE

KOWAKO (ROOSTER) KACHINA

Old Woman had a Taw-Kaw-Kaw Cock which she kept alone so that he would not fight the others. He was very large, like a turkey, with a fine sleek head, and a bristle-brush on his breast like a turkey-cock's, too.

She had him in a corral of tall, close-set stakes, sharp at the top and wattled together with strips of rawhide, like an eagle-cage. It had, too, a wicket fastened with rawhide. Now, try as he would, the Cock could not fly out; and he was hungry for worms and other things that cocks like, for Old Woman was poor and ate mostly grain-foods, and gave the leavings to the Cock.

Now, under the wall near the cage lived a Mouse. He had no old grandmother to feed him, and he was particularly fond of grain food. When the old Cock had eaten his fill, and was sitting in the sun clucking to himself and nodding, Mouse would dart out, steal a bit of pancake or a crumb, and whisk into his hole again. One day the Mouse grew over-bold and took a large piece of bread, and in trying to push it into his hole he made some noise, and, besides, he had to stop and make the doorway larger.

The Cock turned his head just in time to see Mouse's tail there on the ground, wriggling just like worm.

"Hah! It is a worm!" cackled the Cock. He made one peck at Mouse's tail and bit it so hard that he cut it entirely off and swallowed it at one gulp.

Mouse, squeaking "Murder!" scurried into its sleeping-place, and fell to licking his tail until his mouth was all pink, and was all drawn down like a crying woman's; for he loved his long tail. He cried vengence on the Cock for taking away the very mark of his Mousehood.

So, after much planning, he one day put a plaster on his poor tail, and holding it up as a dog does a wounded foot, he went to the edge of his hole and cried in a weak voice to the Taw-Kaw-Kaw Cock:

"Look you, pity, pity! Master of Food Substance,
Of my maiming,
Of my hunger,
I am all but dying. Ah me, pity, ah me!"

Now, the Cock felt sorry for him and proud to be called Master of Plenty, so haughtily he said, "Come in, you poor little thing, and eat all you want." So Mouse went in and ate very little, as became a polite stranger, and, thanking Cock, went back to his hole.

By and by Mouse came back again, bringing with him part of a nut-shell containing fine white meat. Little Mouse said: "Comrade father, let us eat together. I gather this food from yonder high tree, but of all the food I relish yours most. Perhaps you will equally relish mine: let us eat."

No sooner had the Cock tasted this fine food than he chuckled for joy. But there was so little of it that he said, "Comrade little one, do you have plenty of this kind of food?"

"O, yes," replied Mouse. "But, you see, the season is near to an end now, and when I want more nuts I must go and gather them from yonder tree. Look, now! Why do you not go there also?"

"Ah me, I cannot escape, woe to me! My grandmother fastens the wicket tightly with rawhide as soon as she finishes feeding me!"

"Ha! Ha!" exclaimed Mouse. "If that is all, there is nothing easier than to open that." He ran nimbly up the wicket and soon gnawed through the holding-string. "There! Comrade father; push open the door, you are bigger than I, and we will go nutting."

"Thanks this day," cried Cock, and shoving the wicket open, he ran forth cackling and crowing for gladness.

Then Mouse led the way to the tree. Up the trunk he ran, and climbed and climbed until he came to the topmost boughs. "Ha! the nuts are fine and ripe up here!" he shouted.

But Taw-Kaw-Kaw fluttered and flew all in vain. His wings were so worn from trying to get out of his prison that he could not fly even to the lowermost branches. "O, have pity on me, Comrade child! Cut off some of the nuts and throw them down to me!"

"Be patient, be patient, father!" exclaimed Mouse. "I am cracking a big one for you as fast as I can. There, catch it!" And he threw a fat nut close to Cock, who gleefully devoured the kernel, and, without so much as thanks, called for more.

"Wait, father!" said Mouse. "There! stand right under me, so. Now catch it; this is a big one!" And he let fall the nut. It hit the Cock on the head so hard that it bruised the skin off and stunned old Taw-Kaw-Kaw so that he fell over as if dead.

"There, now!" said Mouse. "Lo! Thus healed is my heart!" And he ran back to this cellar satisfied.

Finally Cock opened his eyes. "Ah me, my head!" he exclaimed. His head kept bleeding and swelling, and moaning and staggering he went off to his grandmother.

Hearing him, the grandmother opened the door, and cried, "What now?"

"O, my grandmother, ah me! A great, round, hard seed was dropped on my head by a little creature with a short, one-feathered tail who came and told me that it was good to eat and—oh! My head is all bleeding and swollen! By the light of your favor, bind my wound for me, lest, alas, I die!"

"Serves you right! Why did you leave your place, knowing better?" cried Old Woman. "But you must give me four bristles, or I will not cure you." She slammed the door in his face.

The poor Cock staggered out to find the bristles. He went to his neighbor the Dog, and begged him for four hairs—only four! But Dog said, "You great big noise-maker, bring me some bread, and I will give you the four hairs."

Then the Cock went to the Trader of Foodstuffs and told him his tale. "Well, then, bring me some wood with which I may heat the oven to bake the bread," said the Trader of Foodstuffs.

The Cock then went to some woods near by. "O, ye beloved of the Trees, drop me some dry branches!" And he told his tale. But the Trees shook their leaves and said: "No rain has fallen, and all our branches will soon be dry. Beseech the Waters to give us drink, then we will gladly give you wood."

Then Cock went to a Spring near by, and when he saw his reflection in it, and saw how his head was swollen and that it was growing harder, he again began to lament.

"What is the matter?" murmured the Beloved of the Waters.

Then Cock told them the tale also.

The Spring said, "Place over us four of the plumes from under your wings and the Clouds may see them and send us rain. So Taw-Kaw-Kaw plucked four of his best plumes and set them, one on the northern, one on the western, one on the southern, and one on the eastern border of the Pool. Then the Winds from the four quarters brought the Clouds, and the Clouds gave Rain, and the Trees threw down dry branches, and Cock gathered the fagots and carried them to the Food-maker, who gave him the bread, for which Dog gave him the bristles, and these he took to the old grandmother, who cured his head.

But he had been gone so long that, even though cured, his head remained welted, and ever after there was a great, flabby, blood-red welt on his head and blue marks on his temples where they were bruised so sorely. And the old grandmother said: "It must ever be so. Doing right, keeps right; doing wrong, makes wrong, which, to make right, one must even pay as the sick pay those who cure them."

It is for this reason that ever since that time the medicine-men of that people never give cure without pay; for there is no virtue in medicine of no value. From since then cocks have had blood-red crests of meat on their heads. And even when a hen lays an egg and a Taw-Kaw Cock sees it, he begins to "taw-kaw-kaw" as the ancient of them all did when he saw the brown nut.

As for mice, we know that, ever since the Cock bit off his tail, his children wander wild in the fields; hence field-mice to this day have short tails; and their mouths are all pink, and when you look them in the face they seem always to be crying. ❖

THE CHIRO BIRDS AND THE COYOTE

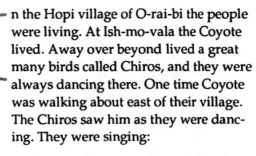

CHIRO MANA

In the Hopi village of O-rai-bi the people were living. At Ish-mo-vala the Coyote lived. Away over beyond lived a great many birds called Chiros, and they were always dancing there. One time Coyote was walking about east of their village. The Chiros saw him as they were dancing. They were singing:

"Coyote, Coyote, to dance is longing,
Coyote upward dances,
Downward dances,
Is called, is called, chi-ro-ro-ro-ro."

Coyote was looking at them and wanted to dance along. "Very well," the Chiros said to him, whereupon each one of them gave him some feathers; one some wing feathers, another some tail feathers, and so on. They made for Coyote a pair of wings and a tail, and put feathers into his body, whereupon Coyote was very happy. "Thanks," he said, "that you have made wings for me. I shall dance with you now."

So they danced, again singing the same song. Coyote danced with them. Now they were flying upward, and arrived somewhere away high up. They crowded around Coyote, and said, "Why, this is my wing; why, this is my tail; why, these are my feathers!" Some of them had given him these things, and now they took everything away from him, and, alas! he began to descend. He arrived at the earth and died. The Chiros laughed at him.

"Thanks," they said, "that you have died, because very often you make raids on some one's property. That is why you were going about again." ❖

THE WAR CHIEFS ABANDON IATIKU

TOTSHA
(HUMMINGBIRD)
KACHINA

Long ago, when the Acoma (Ah-ko-mah) people were still living at a village called White House, Masewi (Mah-seh-wee) and his brother Oyoyewi (O-yo-yeh-wee) lived in the same house with Iatiku (E-ah-tee-koo). Iatiku had an altar in her room with a medicine bowl in front of it.

The two war chiefs used to go into Iatiku's room every night and dance for her until morning. They would dance in front of the altar, so that the water in the medicine bowl would not dry up. Clouds arose from the water in the medicine bowl and spread all over the world, thus insuring abundant rains.

Now, after a time, Iatiku tired of the nightly visits of the two War Brothers, and at last she showed her dislike so plainly that they decided not to return.

So one night, instead of dancing before the altar, they went to each house in the village and collected corn of all kinds and colors. Early the next morning they left the village, traveling toward the north.

After journeying some distance, they selected a spot and dug a deep hole in the ground, which led down into another world. Before descending into this lower world they found Horned Toad and told him that Iatiku had tired of them and their dancing, and that they had decided to leave the village for ten years. They wanted to make the people know that it was they and not Iatiku who brought the rain.

Horned Toad was to sit at the entrance to the hole and guard it during the absence of the two brothers. Masewi caused some flowers to grow about the hole, so that Horned Toad would have food during his long watch. He also supplied Toad with water to drink.

Masewi told Horned Toad to sit at the entrance faithfully and not to move, even though told to do so by some passer-by. "But," he said, "if someone should ask you to open your mouth, then you will do so."

So saying, the brothers went down the hole, way down to a lower world. When they reached the bottom, they went to a place called Flower Mound, where there was a well. Here they started a farm with the seeds they had brought with them. They also brought with them a man to tend the fields. And here they all worked hard and were happy, and stored up much food, for they knew that the people would be starving at the end of the ten years.

Four days after the two war chiefs left, Iatiku was looking for them. The water was going down in her medicine bowl, and all her dancing and all her efforts failed to raise the water in the medicine bowl and to bring rain. Day by day the water went down.

Becoming alarmed, Iatiku asked the Kachina to come to her house to dance. But the water continued to fall in the bowl. At the end of a year the bowl was dry. The spring where the people were accustomed to drink went dry. There was no rain, no snow.

Iatiku appealed to the four Rain Makers of the four cardinal points, but they could do nothing.

Five years passed in this way. Iatiku became desperate. Then she called Humming Bird and asked him to find the two war chiefs.

Humming Bird went to the north, but could find no trace of the two brothers. The next day he went to the west, but was again unsuccessful. On the third day he went to the south, with no success. The fourth day he went to the east, but nothing could be learned of the brothers.

But Humming Bird was not discouraged and set out again, going once more to the north. Attracted by the flowers that Masewi, one of the brothers, had caused to grow to supply Horned Toad with food, Humming Bird came upon him, sitting at the hole.

"Are you there?" Humming Bird greeted Horned Toad.

"Yes," he replied.

Humming Bird asked Horned Toad to move to the north, but he refused. Then he asked him to move to the west, but again he refused. Humming Bird asked him to move to the south, but Toad would not move. Then he asked him to move to the east, but he sat motionless. Then Hummingbird asked Toad to stand up, but Toad would not stand. Then he asked Toad to open his mouth. Horned Toad opened wide his mouth and Humming Bird flew in and right on through him, down the hole.

When he got to the bottom of the hole, Humming Bird went to the west to Flower Mound, where he found the two war chiefs, Masewi and Oyoyewi.

Humming Bird greeted Masewi, and said: "I am looking for you. Iatiku's medicine bowl has dried up."

"What's the matter?" asked Masewi. "Can't Iatiku bring the water and make it rain?"

"No."

Then Humming Bird asked Masewi when he and his brother were going to return. Now, the brothers, being great chiefs, spoke a language that differed somewhat from the Acoma language, so that when Masewi told Humming Bird that they would return in four years, the bird misunderstood him and thought he had said four days. Then they fed Humming Bird, for they had plenty to eat.

Next day Humming Bird set out for the village of White House. When he came to the top of the hole he called out to Horned Toad, "Open your mouth!" Toad did as he was told and Humming Bird flew through and back to Iatiku's house.

"Did you find them?" Iatiku asked.

"Yes," said Humming Bird.

"Where?"

"Down in the lower world. They are coming back in four days," said Humming Bird.

But Iatiku knew that the brothers meant four years, so she began to weep. She wanted to know why they were staying away so long, but Humming Bird could tell her nothing more.

Then Iatiku sent Humming Bird to get some Kachinas to help her. So when they came she sent them to the hole where Horned Toad was, to have them remove Toad by force.

But when they came, Masewi and his brother caused a great cloud to appear over them and it began to hail with great violence. The

Kachinas were compelled to return unsuccessful.

The Kachinas wanted Iatiku to go, but she would not. Just then Swallow happened along. He volunteered to go down the hole to Masewi. So accompanied by Humming Bird he set out.

Humming Bird said to Swallow, "Be careful not to let Horned Toad bite you when you fly through."

When they reached the hole, Swallow asked Horned Toad to open his mouth. Both birds flew through and went down to the lower world. They were welcomed by the two brothers and given something to eat.

Then Swallow said, "I have come to bring you back."

But Masewi said that they did not wish to return yet. After a time, however, they agreed to return on one condition. "If Iatiku sends us something that we really like to eat; if she can guess what it is that we like best and send it to us, we will return," they said.

So the birds set out for the home of Iatiku. Coming up through the hole, they called out to Horned Toad to open his mouth. Humming Bird flew through first. Swallow was a little slow, and when he was flying out of Toad's mouth, Horned Toad bit his tail and pulled four feathers out of the middle. That is why the swallow has a forked tail today.

The birds went to Iatiku's house and told her what the brothers had said. She thought a long while, trying to decide what the brothers would like best to eat. At last she chose some dried berries. She ground them up and made them into four little balls. She wrapped each ball in a corn-husk. Then she inclosed a short downy eagle feather which they always wore on top of their heads.

By this time the four years had almost passed. Some of the people in the village had already died of starvation.

When Iatiku had prepared the gifts, she sent the two birds with them. They went down the hole through Horned Toad's mouth, as before, and handed the gifts to the brothers.

They unwrapped the husks and found the balls of dried berries, which were just what they wanted. So they told the birds to tell Iatiku that they would return in four days, and for her to tell all the people.

Then Masewi gave the birds bags of all kinds of seeds and told them to give them to Iatiku and for her to spread them out before her altar so that they would multiply sufficiently to supply all the people of the village.

Iatiku took the seeds and did as she was told. The next day the seeds had multiplied many times, and she distributed them to the people, who planted them immediately.

On the fourth day Masewi and Oyoyewi came up from the world below. When they came out of the hole they thanked Horned Toad and dismissed him. As soon as they had done this a great cloud formed over all the fields, and it began to rain. It rained for four days and four nights.

Masewi and Oyoyewi returned to their house. Iatiku was very glad to see them. The seeds that the people had planted sprouted and grew. When the rain ceased, four days of sunshine followed. On the fourth night after the rain, the two war chiefs went all through the fields and prayed. Everything began to ripen at once, for the brothers knew that the people were in need of food.

The people then gathered their crops. They set aside a day to visit Masewi and Oyoyewi. Then the people realized that the two brothers possessed great power. That is why the Acoma people today believe in Masewi and Oyoyewi. ❖

How the Twin War Gods Stole the Thunder-Stone and the Lightning-Shaft

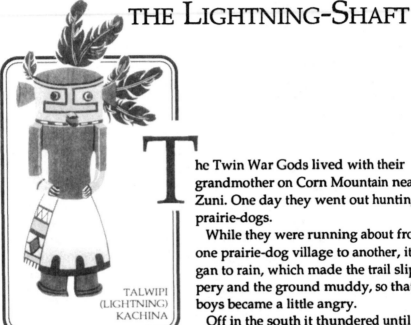

TALWIPI
(LIGHTNING)
KACHINA

The Twin War Gods lived with their grandmother on Corn Mountain near Zuni. One day they went out hunting prairie-dogs.

While they were running about from one prairie-dog village to another, it began to rain, which made the trail slippery and the ground muddy, so that the boys became a little angry.

Off in the south it thundered until the earth trembled, and the lightning-shafts flew about the red-bordered clouds until the two brothers were blinded by it. Presently the young brother smoothed his brow, then jumped up and cried out:

"Elder brother, let us go to the Land of Everlasting Summer and steal from the Rain Gods their Thunder and Lightning! I think it would be fine fun to do that sort of thing we have just been looking at and listening to."

The elder brother was somewhat more curious; but he liked the idea, so he said; "Let us take our prairie-dogs home to grandmother, that she shall have something to eat meanwhile, and we will think about going tomorrow morning."

The next morning, bright and early, the Twins started out. In vain the old grandmother called rather crossly after them, "Where are you going now?" She could get no satisfaction, for she knew the Twins lied when they called back, "O, we are only going to hunt more prairie-dogs!" It is true that they played around in the plains about Corn Mountain a little while, as if looking for prairie-dogs. Then they sped away toward that beautiful country of the corals, the Land of Everlasting Summer.

At last they came to the House of the Beloved Gods themselves. That red house was a wondrous terrace, rising wall after wall, and step after step, like a high mountain, grand and stately. But the walls were so steep and smooth and high that the skill and power of the little War Gods were of no use. They could not climb up.

"What shall we do?" asked the younger brother.

"Go home," said the elder, "and mind our own affairs."

"O, no!" urged the younger. "I have it, elder brother. Let us hunt up our grandfather, the Centipede."

"Good!" exclaimed the elder. "That's a happy thought, my younger brother."

So at once they laid down their bows, their quivers of mountain-lion skin, their shields, and other things, and set about turning over all the flat stones they could find. Presently, lifting a stone with all their strength, they found under it the very old fellow they sought. He doubled himself and covered his eyes from the brightness of the daylight. He did not much like being thus disturbed, even by his grandchildren, the War Gods, in the middle of his noonday nap, and was by no means polite to them. But they prodded him a little in the side, and said: "Now, grandfather, look here! We are in difficulty, and there is no one in the wide world who can help us out as you can."

The old Centipede was flattered by this remark. He unrolled himself and viewed the Twins with a look which he intended to be reproachful. "Ah, my grandchildren," said he, "what are you up to now? Are you trying to get yourselves into trouble, as usual? No doubt of it! I will help you all I can, but the consequences be on your own heads!"

"That's right, grandfather, that's right? No one in the world could help us as you can," said one of the boys. "The fact is, we want to get hold of the thunder-stone and the lightning-shaft which the Rain Gods up there in the great house keep and guard so carefully, we understand. Now, in the first place, we cannot climb up the wall; in the second place, if we did, we would probably have a fuss with the Rain Gods in trying to steal those things. Therefore, we want you to help up, if you will."

"With all my heart, my boys!" answered Centipede; "but I should advise you to run along home to your grandmother, and let those things alone."

"O, nonsense! We are only going to play a little while with the thunder and lightning," they replied.

"All right," replied the old Worm, "sit here and wait for me." He wriggled himself and stirred about, and his countless legs were more countless than ever with rapid motions as he ran toward the walls of that stately terrace. A vine could not have run up more closely, nor a bird more rapidly. If one foot slipped, another held on. So the old Centipede wriggled himself up the sides and over the roof, and down into the great sky-hole. Scorning the ladder, which he feared might creak, he went along, head-downward, on the ceiling to the end of the room over the altar, ran down the side, and approached that most forbidden of places, the altar of the Rain Gods themselves.

The beloved gods were sitting there with their heads bowed in meditation so deep that they heard not the faint scuffle of Centipede's feet as he wound himself down into the altar and stole the thunder-stone. He took it in his mouth (which was larger than the mouths of centipedes are now) and carried it silently, heavy as it was, up the way he had come, over the roof, down the wall, and back to the flat stone where he made his home, and where the Twin War Gods were eagerly awaiting him.

"Here he comes!" cried the younger brother. "And he's got it! By my war-bonnet, he's got it!"

The old grandfather threw the thunder-stone down. It began to sound, but one of the boys grabbed it and smothered its thunderous noise. "Good! Good!"

"Hold on!" cried the younger brother. "You didn't bring both. What can we do with the one without the other?"

"O, hush!" cried the old Worm. "I know what I am about!" And before they could say any more he was off again. Before long he returned, carrying in his mouth the shaft of lightning with its gleaming point.

"Good!" cried the War Gods. The younger brother caught up the lightning, almost forgetting his weapons, and started on a full run for Corn Mountain, followed by his brother, who brought along the thunder-stone, which he found was a great deal heavier than he had supposed.

So swift and powerful were these Gods of War that before long they reached the home of their grandmother on the top of Corn Mountain. They had carefully concealed the thunder-stone and the shaft of lightning meanwhile, and had taken care to provide themselves with a few prairie-dogs so that their grandmother would not know what they had really been doing.

Back in the mountains of Everlasting Summer still sat the Rain Gods, not knowing what Grandfather Centipede had done.

Not long after they arrived, the young War Gods became eager to try their new playthings. They poked at each other, and whispered a great deal, so that their grandmother began to suspect they were about to play some rash joke or other. Presently she spied the point of lightning gleaming under the younger brother's jacket.

"Demons!" she cried. "By the moon! You have stolen the thunderstone and the lightning-shaft from the Gods of Rain themselves! Go this instant and return them, and never do such a thing again!" she cried. Making a quick step for the fireplace, she picked up the wooden poker with which to beat them, but they whisked out of the room and ran into another. They slammed the door in their grandmother's face and braced it. Clearing away a lot of rubbish that was lying around the rear room, they hid themselves in one end. Nodding and winking at each other, they cried out, "Now, then!" The younger brother let go the lightning-shaft, the other rolled the thunder-stone. The lightning hissed through the air and far out into the sky, and returned. The thunder-stone rolled and rumbled until it shook the mountain.

"Great fun!" cried the boys, rubbing their sides in delight. "Do it again!" So again they sent forth the lightning-shaft and rolled the thunder-stone.

And now the gods in Summerland arose and breathed toward the skies. The winds rose and the rains fell like rivers from the clouds, dashing violently upon the roof of the poor old grandmother's house.

Those reckless boys kept on playing the thunder-stone and lightning-shaft without the slightest regard for the awful commotion they were raising all through the skies and all over Corn Mountain.

But nowhere else as above the house where their poor old grandmother lived, fell the torrent of rain, and there alone, of course, flashed the lightning and rolled the thunder.

Soon the water poured through the roof of the house, but move the things as the old grandmother would, she could not keep them dry. Scold the boys as she would, she could not make them stop. No, they would only go on with their play more violently than ever, exclaiming: "What has she to say, anyway? It won't hurt her to get a good ducking, and this is fun!"

By and by the waters rose so high that they quenched the fire. Soon the waters rose still higher, so that the War Gods had to paddle around half under the flood. Still they kept flashing the lightning and rolling the thunder-stone.

The old grandmother scolded harder and harder, but after a while ceased and climbed to the top of the fireplace, where she began again. But the boys heeded her not, only saying: "Let her yell! Let her scold! This is fun!" At last they began to take the old grandmother's scolding as a matter of course, and allowed nothing but the water to interrupt their sport.

The water rose so high, finally, that they were near drowning. Then they climbed to the roof, but still they kept on making lightning and thunder.

"By the bones of the dead! Why did we not think to come here before? It's ten times as fine up here. See him shoot!" cried one to the other, as the lightning sped through the sky, ever returning.

"Hear it rumble and roll!" cried the other, as the thunder bellowed and grumbled.

But no sooner had the Twins begun their sport than the rain fell in a vast sheet all about them. It was not long before the house was so full that the old grandmother knocked her poor head on the rafters in trying to keep it above the water. She gulped water, gasped, coughed, strangled, and shrieked to no purpose.

"What a fuss our old grandmother is making, to be sure!" cried the boys. And they kept on until the water had completely filled the room, and the grandmother's cries finally ceased.

Now the lightning grew so hot and the thunder so terrific that the boys, drawing a long breath and thinking of the fun they had had, flung the lightning-shaft and the thunder-stone into the sky, where, flashing and rattling away, they finally disappeared over the mountains in the south.

Then the clouds rolled away and the sun shone out. The boys, wet to the skin, and tired and hungry, looked around.

"Goodness! the water is running out of the windows of our house! This is a pretty mess we are in! Grandmother! Grandmother!" they shouted. "Open the door and let us in!"

But the only sound the boys heard was that of rushing water. They sat down on the roof and waited for the water to get lower. Then they climbed down and pounded open the door, and the water came streaming out, carrying their poor old grandmother with it. Her eyes were staring, her hair all tangled and muddied, and her arms and legs as stiff as sticks.

"O, ye gods! ye gods!" the two boys exclaimed. "We have killed our own grandmother! Poor old grandmother, who scolded us so hard and loved us so much! Let us bury her here in front of the door as soon as the water has run away."

So as soon as it became dry enough, there they buried her. In less than four days a strange plant grew up on that spot, and on its little branches, amid its bright green leaves, hung long, pointed pods of fruit, as red as the fire on the breast of the redbird.

"It is well," said the boys, as they stood one day looking at this plant. "Let us scatter the seeds abroad, that men may find and plant them. It seems it was not without good cause that in our sport we thoughtlessly killed our old grandmother, for out of her heart there sprung a plant into the fruits of which has flowed the color as well as the fire of her scolding tongue. And if we have lost our grandmother, whom we loved much, but who loved us more, men have gained a new food, which, though it burn them, shall please them more than the heat of her scoldings please us!"

Poor old grandmother! Men will little dream when they eat chile peppers that the seed of them first arose from the fiery heart of the grandmother of the Twin War Gods.

Then the Twins seized the pepper-pods and crushed them between their hands, with an exclamation of pleasure at their sharp odor. They cast the seed abroad, and here and there they took root. So the plants which sprang from the seeds being afterward found by men, were looked upon as good and were cultivated, as they are to this day in the pepper gardens of Zuni.

Ever since that time, around the mountain wherein lived the Twin War Gods with their grandmother, the lightning flashes and the thunder plays, and the rain falls there most often.

It is said by some that the two boys, when asked how they stole the lightning-shaft and the thunder-stone, told on their poor old grandfather, the Centipede. The Beloved Gods of the Rain gave him the lightning-shaft to handle in another way, and it so burned and shriveled him that he became small, as you can see by looking at any of the many centipedes today, which are not only small, but appear like a well-toasted bit of buckskin fringed at the edges. ❖

WHY ANTS ARE SO THIN

HOPI
SHALAKO
MAIDEN

The busy little Ant village in Hopiland was busier than ever, for the great Ant Chief had told everyone that in four days all the little Ant children between the ages of seven and eleven would be made members of the Kachina Society. The mothers were busy grinding corn, and getting the children ready, and telling them not to be frightened, for you know, the children are all whipped by the Whipping Kachinas when they are initiated into the Kachina Society, so they are very much afraid. The Kachinas were busy fixing their masks and costumes, and everyone was doing his bit for the great day.

At last the great day arrived. The two Whipping Kachinas went a short distance from the village to put on their gay costumes. Other Ants made sand pictures on the floor of the kiva, as the large underground room is called. They made these pictures by sifting different-colored earths and sands through their fingers, just as the Hopi Indians do when they are getting ready for a dance. Then the Ants began to bring to the kiva their children who where to be initiated.

When the little Ant children had all passed through the hole in the roof of the kiva, which is its only doorway, and climbed down the ladder, they stood shivering with fright. The Kachina priest of the Ants told them the story that is always told to Hopi children when they are initiated. Now everything that is told the children in this ceremony is a secret, and they are punished severely if they tell any of the younger children.

Four little Ant Clowns, called Ko-yem-shi, now appeared at the hole in the roof of the kiva, and quickly and merrily went down the ladder, dancing and singing and clowning. All the children laughed at their antics.

While all this was going on in the kiva, one of the Ants had been sitting on a rock outside, and when the other Ant Kachinas had finished what they were doing in the kiva, this Ant swung one forefoot as a signal for the Whipping Kachinas to come. The Whipping Kachinas at once came running to the kiva, circled around it several times and then entered it, taking their places opposite the sand picture on the floor.

The Whipping Kachinas then said to the Ant god-parents, "Bring your children up for their whipping, for they have been bad, and must be whipped!"

The little Ant children commenced to whimper, but the god-mother and god-father Ants took their god-children up to the Kachinas, to whom they gave a pinch of cornmeal. The Whipping Kachinas then whipped the god-mother and god-father. But they whipped the little Ant children so hard that they almost cut them through the middle of their bodies. These Ant Kachinas did not know that the Indian Kachinas do not whip the little Indian children hard, so when they saw what they had done, the Ant Kachinas became frightened and ran away.

So that is the reason, the Hopi say, why ants are now so thin in the middle of their bodies, because they were almost cut in two at that initiation. ❖

HOW RATTLESNAKES CAME TO BE WHAT THEY ARE

CHUA (RATTLESNAKE) KACHINA

Long, long ago there lived at Up-Above-Place, as live there now, many Rattlesnakes; but then they were men and women, only of a rattlesnake kind.

One day the little children of one of the houses there wished to go out to play at sliding down the sand-banks south of Bitter Pond on the other side of the Zuni river. So they cried out to their parents, "Let us go, O, mother, grandmother, father! and take our little sister to play on the sunny side of the sand-banks."

"My children," said the mother, "go if you wish, but be very careful of your little sister; for she is very young. Carry her gently on your shoulders, and place her where she will be safe, for she is very small and helpless."

"O, yes!" cried the children. "We love our little sister, don't we, little one?" said they, turning to the baby girl. Then they took her up in their blankets, and carried her on their shoulders out to the sunny side of the sand-banks; and there they began to play at sliding one after another.

The little girl, immensely delighted with their sport, toddled out from the place where they had set her down, just as one of the girls was speeding down the side of the sand-hill. The little creature ran, clapping her hands and laughing, to catch her sister as she came, and the elder one, trying in vain to stop herself, called out to her to be careful; but she was a little thing, and knew not the meaning of her sister's warning. Alas! The elder one slid down upon her, knocked her over and rolled her in the sand, crushing her so that she died, and rolling her out very small.

The children all gathered around their little sister, and cried and cried. Finally they took her up tenderly, and placing her on their shoulders, sang as they went slowly toward home:

> "Rattlesnake little-little!
> Rattlesnake little-little!
> Alas, we bear her!
> Alas, we bear her!"

As they approached the village of the Rattlesnakes, the mother of the little one looked out and saw them coming and heard their song.

"O, my children! my children!" she cried. "You foolish little ones, did I not tell you to beware and be careful? O, my children!" Then she exclaimed — rocking herself to and fro, and wriggling from side to side at the same time, casting her hands into the air, and sobbing wildly:

> "O, alas! our little maiden!
> O, alas! our little maiden!
> Ala-a-a-a-s!"

Then she fell in a swoon, still wriggling, to the ground.

When the old grandmother saw them coming, she too said:

> "O, alas! our little maiden!"

As one after another in the village saw the beloved little child brought home, mutilated and dead, each cried out as the others had cried:

> "O, alas! our little maiden!"

Then all swooned away. The children also who were bringing the little one joined in the cry of woe, and swooned away. And when they all returned to life, they could not arise, but went wriggling along the ground, faintly crying, as rattlesnakes wriggle and cry to this day.

So you see that once (as was the case with many, if not all, of the animals) the Rattlesnakes were a people, and a splendid people, too. Therefore, we kill them not needlessly, nor waste the lives even of other animals without cause. ❖

NOTES

WHY KACHINAS WEAR EAGLE FEATHERS / Page 6

Prayer-sticks, offered by the Zunis to the sun, the moon, and the rain-makers, are made with downy feathers of the eagle, the most sacred of birds. After planting these sticks, the one who offers them to the Sky gods must not eat any animal food for four days. The down feather of the eagle is considered to belong to the Sun Priest, because he always plants to the sun. The other priests use it when rain is urgently needed because the down suggests the fleecy clouds that gather on the horizon before the rain.

For a long time the crops of the Hopi were not good, but when the people began to use many eagle feathers on their prayer-sticks, the crops became better and rabbits increased. When the men are gathering rattlesnakes for the Snake Dance, the Hopi tame the reptile by brushing over it with two eagle-feathers until it straightens out and tries to escape, when they seize it quickly by the neck. The Twin War Gods of the Hopi are supposed to travel on the rainbow or on the downy feather of an eagle, and thus move about as fast as lightning.

A very beautiful Eagle Dance is performed by the Tewa Indians of New Mexico and has been adopted by other Pueblo tribes as well.

HOW BEES LEARNED TO FLY AND HOW PEACHES BECAME SWEET / Page 10

Momo, the Bee Kachina of the Hopi, carries a tiny bow and arrows. In the dance he imitates the hum of the bee and goes from one spectator to another, shooting blunt arrows at them. The children become frightened, so to still their cries, Momo Kachina squirts a little water on the supposed wound.

The Zuni Indians mix honey with the black paint they use on the Kachina masks to make it shiny. They believe that the bees, flying in all directions, will bring the winds from each direction which will bring the rain. They use the honey because the bees come on beautiful days and the children like to catch them. So they pray with the bees' honey. The honey is thick, and they want the rain to come thick and soak the earth.

The Indians also used honey as medicine to quiet crying children, and they gave it to babies when they were teething.

It should be remembered that peaches were not known to the Pueblo Indians before the Spaniards went among them, hence the tale dates from historic times, probably after the year 1629, when the first missionaries began to christianize the Zuni and Hopi Indians.

HOW THE DEER GOT THEIR RED EYES / Page 12

Dr. Elsie Chew Parsons, who recorded this myth, says that when the Hunt Chief of Isleta pueblo holds his ceremony after the harvest, he blows smoke into his medicine bowl, then puffs smoke toward the mountains to blind the deer, and he whistles to draw in the deer. He then makes a circle of pollen on the ground, leaving an opening at the east. In his hand is a goose feather, and he calls out like a wolf. Then when someone opens the door, the Hunt Chief sings, and in comes a man dressed as a deer with big horns. The deer walks into the circle of pollen, which the chief then closes. The deer snorts, the chief taps him on the forehead, and he drops as if dead. Among the Isleta Indians success in hunting is a test usually imposed on suitors for the hand of a fairmaiden, and several suitors fail because they neglect to offer sacred prayer-meal to the game animals.

According to Zuni tradition, the Twin War Gods made Wolf the Guardian of the East. He is one of the Beast Gods to whom the War Gods entrusted the secrets of making and using medicine for the cure of disease, and they told the Beast Gods to teach these secrets to others.

In Indian tales it is only natural that animals should be thought of as killing deer and weaker animals, just as white men often go out hunting only for the purpose of killing.

THE FOSTER CHILD OF THE DEER / Page 14

The Zuni Indians and others believe the sun is the source of all life. It is, therefore, called "our Sun Father." Each morning as the sun sends his first level beams striking across the houses, his people come out to meet him with prayers and offerings. Men and women stand before their doors, facing the east, their hands full of corn-meal which is offered to the sun, with prayers for long life and abundant crops.

The Sun Priest, who holds his power directly from the Sun Father, is the most revered and most holy man in Zuni, and is held responsible for the welfare of the community. As Priest of the Sun he is keeper of the calendar. He sets the dates for the solstices, at which time there are elaborate festivals in honor of the Sun Father, so that he may shower his blessings on the people.

The naming of a Zuni child takes place on the tenth day after its birth. Just as the first rays of the sun appear, the child is held up toward it and sacred corn-meal is cast toward the Sun Father, when long life is asked for the infant.

Indians do not needlessly kill animals. Only when in need of food or clothing do they go hunting. Then they offer prayer-meal and prayer-sticks to the spirit of the deer and other game animals, and the hunters divide the meat, giving certain parts to the other animals, burying certain parts for the earth, and giving certain portions to the Hunt Chief and the Town Chief, and some to his relatives. To do this insures good luck in the next hunt.

During the time the hunter is away, the wife is advised to clean house, to plaster the walls, to keep herself very clean, not to scold the children, not to quarrel with the neighbors or gad about among them. When the deer is brought in, it is covered with a woman's shawl, with beads around its neck. This the woman does in return for the deerskin she is to have.

In early times the Zuni hunters spread out in a great circle, covering many miles, and gradually closing in, driving the deer into a kind of corral made of trees and brush. Then the hunters shot the deer, which now were helpless.

TIHKUYI CREATES THE GAME ANIMALS / Page 21

The rabbit played a most important part in the life of the Hopi. While large game, such as antelope, deer, and mountain sheep, were occasionally captured, the task was so difficult that rabbits furnished by far the greater portion of their meat, and the fur was used for clothing. After a boy has killed his first rabbit, he is initiated as a hunter. Four days after the initiation, a rabbit hunt is announced, and the boy is dressed and painted like an initiate into the Kachina order, and becomes chief of the hunt.

So the Hopi appeal to the Snow Kachina for snow in the mountains, that it may feed the spring freshets, that the people may have plenty of water and that the hunters will have success in the hunt, because when it snows, they can follow the tracks of the animals.

At the Winter Solstice ceremony, offerings are left at the shrine of Tihkuyi (Tee-kuh-yee), who created the game animals, that she may increase the supply of game. When a hunting party is organized, Tihkuyi is asked to give the hunters permission to kill her children.

THE K'YAKLU BEING AND THE DUCK / Page 24

When K'yaklu was at the Sacred Lake, Pautiwa ("god-chief") directed him to prepare the people for a visit from the gods. So K'yaklu was carried from the Sacred Lake to Halona Itiwana, a pueblo then inhabited across the river from the present Zuni, on the backs of the Koyemashi, and after repeating to the people the story of their emergence from the lower worlds and of their wanderings in search of the middle of the earth, he told them to build six kivas or ceremonial chambers, in which to receive the gods eight days later. After eight days Pautiwa and the other gods came and instructed them how to form a fraternity in imitation of the gods. Men and gods were then assigned to the six kivas. But after the dance had been observed several times, it was noticed that many deaths occurred after each performance, so the gods decided that it would be better to have their faces represented by masks, and to have certain men take the place of gods. Since that time the Pueblos have had masked Kachina dances.

All male children are initiated into the fraternity of God Personators in a ceremony which occurs every fourth year.

The ceremony is held in March or April, depending upon the moon. Eight days before the actual whipping of the children in the initiation, the man personating K'yaklu is carried into the village on the backs of the Koyemashi, one relieving the other. K'yaklu carries a stuffed duck in his hand, and the Koyemashi sing as they approach the village before sunrise. Being a very sacred personage, K'yaklu does not put his feet upon the ground. As he goes from kiva to kiva to announce the coming of the gods in eight days, and also to repeat the story of creation and migration, one of the Koyemashi carries him up the ladder and deposits him upon a blanket. He then descends into the kiva.

The ceremony lasts from sunrise to sunrise, and at daybreak K'yaklu is carried back toward the sacred lake, whence he is supposed to have come.

After K'yaklu leaves, the head men of each kiva select those who are to personate the gods in the forthcoming initiation ceremony.

The Tewa Pueblo Indians use duck feathers, together with other feathers, in making prayer-sticks for use in the initiation into certain societies, because Duck flies in all directions and will assist in carrying the prayers to the gods in every quarter.

THE RETURN OF THE CORN MAIDS / Page 29

Corn is very sacred to the Indians, especially the Pueblos. Not only is it the most important food, but, next to prayer-sticks with feathers attached, it is the most acceptable offering to the gods. Songs sung when corn is ground are sacred, and indeed everything connected with the handling of corn is sacred. Corn-meal is offered to the sun each morning by the Sun Priest. Medicine-men are sometimes given large baskets of corn-meal as their fee for performing a healing ceremony for a sick person.

Sacred prayer-meal, made of coarse corn-meal containing ground white shell and turquoise, is used in ceremonies. The Summer Cacique prays for rain and growing crops, using in his prayers meal made of blue corn, symbolic of the blue summer sky; the Winter Cacique prays for snow and fertile seeds, using meal of white corn, symbolic of snow-covered fields. In the Scalp ceremony the priest mounted to four housetops, leaving a grain of black corn on each, "to make his road dark" to the enemy.

Parts of the corn are used for making paint for use on Kachina masks and on the bodies of Kachina personators.

Pautiwa is chief of the masked gods or Kachinas. He is a magnificent person, possessing great beauty, dignity, and kindliness. The moment he appears in the plaza at the close of the solstice ceremonies in Zuni, all merrymaking ceases and the people watch this splendid god approach with hushed reverence. At the New Year ceremony, Pautiwa comes to give his orders for the coming year. He appoints those who are to impersonate the gods in the great Shalako ceremony in early winter. It is after the Shalako ceremony that the Corn Maids are brought in and Pautiwa comes with them, bringing water in a gourd from the Sacred Lake. The Corn Maids symbolize fertility, and the water symbolizes plentiful rains.

The Newekwe mentioned in the myth are a fraternity of sacred clowns.

HOW THE CORN PESTS WERE TRAPPED

Very often in their stories the Zuni Indians refer to the "ancients," or "old ones," meaning their ancestors.

The town called the "Middle Ant Hill of the World" was Halona, or, more fully, Halona Itiwana, which was situated across the Zuni river from the present Zuni pueblo. Halona was abandoned at the time of the great rebellion of the Pueblo Indians against Spanish authority in 1680 and was never again occupied.

In ancient times, the Divine Ones, wishing that the world should be well guarded by those keen of sight and scent, changed the medicine-men who came to this world into Beast Gods. They changed one into the Bear to guard the west. One was converted into the Mountain Lion to guard the north. Another was made into the Badger to guard the south. Another was transformed into the Wolf to preside over the east. A fifth was changed into the Eagle to guard the upper regions, and another became the Mole to guard the lower regions. Others were changed into Rattlesnakes and Ants to preside with wisdom over the earth.

The Bear is the most powerful healing agency of the medicine-men, who, therefore, imitate the Bear in their healing ceremonies; but only the oldest and most learned of the medicine-men are allowed to draw over their hands the bear paws, thus impersonating them.

Old Hopi medicine-men advise those who are just becoming medicine-men not to go among the people to cure them, but to wait until the people come for help in time of sickness. If the first one to come for help is of the Bear Clan, that is best. In this case especially the young medicine-man must make every effort to cure him, for if he succeeds in curing this first patient, he will always be successful.

During the final ceremony of the societies at the Winter Solstice in Zuni, when the sick are cured in public ceremonies, the medicine-men undergo a complete change of personality. At that time they rush about, uttering the cries of the animals they represent. They are very much feared. It is especially the function of the bear to give the power of magical impersonation. Since disease is generally caused by a witch who injects foreign bodies into the patient, the Zunis believe the surest way to cure is to locate and remove the foreign substance. The medicine-man locates this either by use of a crystal or by partaking of a drug that produces a vision. When the cause of the trouble has been located, the medicine-man sucks at the spot and draws out the foreign substance, usually a small pebble, which he spits into a bowl. Though this is a very clever bit of sleight-of-hand, the medicine-men have a great knowledge of herbs, and perform many cures with their medicines and by singing.

Among the Hopi the fat of the bear and of the mountain lion is eaten and smeared over the body in cases of smallpox. Bears were never the object of a hunt, and the meat was used only when one happened to be killed accidentally. The Navajos do not kill a bear except under the stress of great hunger, and then only by asking the bear's pardon.

THE COCK AND THE MOUSE / Page 37

Frank Hamilton Cushing, who lived among the Zunis for several years for the purpose of studying their customs and language, related to them the story of the Cock and the Mouse published in Thomas F. Crane's "Italian Popular Tales." Years later, a Zuni surprised Cushing by retelling the same story, or rather the Zuni version of it, which accounts for the origin of the cock's comb, the short-tufted tails of field-mice, and other things that do not occur in the Italian story, which to the Zunis seemed very incomplete.

While the Pueblo Indians had flocks of turkeys in ancient times, they did not have chickens until after the Spaniards went among them nearly four hundreds years ago, hence their occurrence in ceremonies and in the form of Kachina dolls, shows their modern origin. In Zuni a chicken is called taw-kaw-kaw, because of the sound it makes.

The Cock appears in the Hopi Soyalanu ceremony, at which is celebrated the return of the Sun God as leader of the Kachinas. Many other birds appear in this ceremony, impersonated by men, who dress in the feathers, wings, and tail of the birds. They wear elaborate bird masks, which are all freshly painted.

During the dance the sun-shield bearer personates a warrior contending with enemies and dashes his shield in the faces of groups of men who take the part of warriors who surge against him again and again as if in attack. Many fall down exhausted before this ordeal ends. The make-believe attacks and repulses of these men upon the shield-bearer typify the assaults of hostile gods upon the sun, who at the end is victorious over them all, and returns to bless the people.

THE CHIRO BIRDS AND THE COYOTE / Page 41

At the Powamu, or Coming of the Kachinas ceremony, in Hopi-land, which occurs in February, the Chiro Mana, or Chiro Kachina Maiden, and Kerwan, a male Kachina, distribute bean sprouts which have been artificially raised in the kivas. They bring the sprouts out in a flat basket, which they carry between them, and distribute to all the people.

Within four days each man must gather some sand in a box and plant a few beans, each in the kiva belonging to his clan. If a man fails to do this, it is taken as a sign that his crop in the coming season will fail to ripen. They tend these miniature crops for eight days, and on the ninth day they harvest. If anyone accidentally breaks a plant before the harvest, the Whipping Kachinas are called in and the offender is whipped with yucca-leaves.

While waiting for the plants to grow in the kivas, the men are busy making dolls, representing Kachinas, for the girls, and rattles and shinny-balls for their boys, and moccasins for all.

After the crops have been harvested, each man binds his plants in small sheaves, making one for each of his young children, and to each sheaf he attaches the gifts made for the particular child to whom it will be given. The Kachinas then distribute them.

The Pueblo Indians, like other Western Indians, have many coyote stories, in most of which Coyote, who thinks himself so sly, is outwitted by other animals.

THE WAR CHIEFS ABANDON IATIKU / Page 42

Masewi and Oyoyewi are the twin war gods of the Acoma people. They are the patron gods of the Warriors' Society and of the war chiefs. To the Acoma people they symbolize courage, strength, and virtue. They are also represented in mythology as great rainmakers.

Iatiku is very sacred and of the greatest importance. She is the symbol of life itself and is called the mother of all Indians. A short prayer and a bit of food are offered to Iatiku before each meal.

The Humming Bird is supposed to carry messages from the Indians to the spirits. The

Tewa Indians make offerings consisting of sacred meal, specially ground for the purpose and carried in small pouches or in cloth packets, and bunches of feathers bound with cotton spring, each bunch containing a feather of a goose, a turkey, a magpie, an eagle, an oriole, a summer warbler, and a duck. These messages to the spirits are supposed to be carried by Humming Bird, Eagle, and Hawk. The meal is tossed in small pinches, either in the general direction of the supposed home of the deity addressed, or directly on the sacred objects representing the spirits.

In the Apache creation myth, Humming Bird was sent about the world in the very beginning to note how its creation progressed.

There is a Zuni myth in which Humming Bird goes to the spring near the village of K'iakima, where he throws off his humming-bird coat and becomes a handsome youth. The daughter of a great priest, whom all the young men of the village were wooing incessantly, came to the spring for water. The Humming Bird youth asked her for a drink, which she gave him. They fell in love with each other. The next day, when the Humming Bird youth went to the spring, he took with him some honey and sunflower pollen, which he gave to the maiden. The maiden's family liked the food so much that they decided she should marry the youth, so that he could always provide them with such delicious food. So they married. Humming Bird youth, though he had discarded his humming-bird coat, kept it hidden near by in case of need.

The young men of the village were very jealous of Humming Bird youth, so they plotted to get rid of him. Though these plots were cleverly laid, Humming Bird youth outwitted the young men because of his humming-bird coat and the help he received from the animals, his friends. In the end the young men realized how great Humming Bird youth was, so they called him father and his wife they called mother, which are terms of reverence among the Indians.

HOW THE TWIN WAR GODS STOLE THE THUNDER-STONE AND THE LIGHTNING-SHAFT / Page 47

The twin children of the Sun were, in the days of creation, the friendly guardians of men; but when the world became filled with envy and war, they were changed by the eight gods of the storms into warriors more powerful than all monsters, gods, or men. They are now known as the Twin War Gods and are ever getting into mischief or seeking scenes of contention; for whatever is deathly and dreadful to others, is lively and delightful to them.

In the story the twin boys unintentionally drowned their grandmother by playing the lightning-shaft and thunder-stone too long. They repented of their awful deed, and buried her. But good often comes from evil, for over her dead grave chile peppers sprang up and have afforded to the people one of the favorite seasonings for their food.

The Twin War Gods established the Priesthood of the Bow, or War Society, in the very early days of the world when the Zuni people were looking for the middle place at which to settle, and strife and contention rose among them. The Priests of the Bow guarded the women and children and the old ones on their long journeys.

Lightning and thunder can be summoned by medicine-men and directed at will. Many of the songs and dances are for the purpose of bringing rain. If it thunders and lightnings, rain is sure to follow, so the medicine-men have their lightning-sticks and thunder-stones.

WHY ANTS ARE SO THIN / Page 53

Ants were sacred to the ancient people of Zuni, for they believed that the ants destroyed the footprints of the warriors from the eyes of the enemy, who therefore could not follow them. The Zunis now have their Ant fraternity, or brotherhood. When in very ancient times the Zunis were seeking the middle of the world, there to settle in order to avoid earthquakes, they reached the present Zuni and there built the pueblo of Halona Itiwana (Hah'-lo-nah Ee'-tee-wah-na), the "Middle Ant-hill of the World." To this day a shrine marks the exact middle according to Zunis belief.

When the Powamu (Po'-wah-moo) ceremony is performed by the Hopi, then is the time for boys between the ages of eleven and seventeen to be initiated by flogging. The Whipping Kachinas go into the street and call in a loud voice in front of the houses, "We have come to whip your children!" A mother answers that she does not want her children whipped. But one of the Whipping Kachinas says they must be whipped, because the children have been bad. The mother asks to be whipped first, so they give her four lashes on the back with a bunch of yucca leaves. The Whipping Kachinas then go back to the kiva, or underground ceremonial chamber, and the god-parents bring each child before them to be whipped. The god-parents give a pinch of sacred meal to the Kachinas, then bend to receive the four lashes themselves before the child is whipped. The children are greatly frightened, but all must go through this initiation to be purified. They then become members of the tribe and are told the secrets of the Kachinas. The children are warned never to tell the Kachina secrets to the younger children; if they disobey, they are severely punished.

The Koyemashi are a body of sacred clowns who impersonate the malformed beings who were born when the earth was new and the Zuni Indians were searching for the middle place of the world in which Zuni Indians were searching for the middle place of the world in which to settle to be free from earthquakes. There are ten of these grotesque masked beings who have knobs on their heads, protruding, puckered mouths, and with bodies painted with pinkish clay. The Koyemashi assist at all Kachina dances, and act as clowns and play games when the Kachinas are not dancing. They are very sacred personages, and the most dangerous of the Kachinas, therefore the people never refuse them anything, for to do so would bring bad luck.

When the Koyemashi come for the first time, which is usually after the summer solstice, they pass every house in the village, and the women throw water on them from the housetops to induce rain to come.

HOW RATTLESNAKES CAME TO BE WHAT THEY ARE / Page 55

Every year the Hopi Indians hold a Snake Dance, which is an elaborate prayer for rain, in which the reptiles are gathered from the valley, intrusted with the prayers of the people, and then given their liberty to bear these petitions to the gods who can bring the blessing of copious rains to the parched and arid farms.

Boys of the Rattlesnake clan of the Hopi, and sons of Rattlesnake clansmen, as well as those who, having been bitten by a snake or afflicted with a disease believed to have been caused by one, have been cured by a Snake Priest, are obliged to join either the Snake or the Antelope fraternity.

The initiation takes place in early boyhood, and the child is given his choice of entering the Snake fraternity at once, or of joining the Antelopes for a time. Later, as a young man, he will become a Snake priest, provided he is brave enough, and as a very old man he will return to the ranks of the Antelopes. The boys are given their choice of joining either the Snakes or the Antelopes. If they are afraid of snakes, they frankly declare it and join the Antelopes. Later, if they feel courageous enough, they join the Snakes.

Many young men do not like to handle snakes, for in the dance they are carried in the mouth, wrapped around their necks and waists, and carried in the hands, so they remain in the Antelope fraternity, and dance with the Snake men, but do not handle the snakes.

WORKS CONSULTED

Bunzel, Ruth L. Introduction to Zuni Ceremonialism. Zuni Origin Myths. Zuni Ritual Poetry. Zuni. Katchinas. 47th Report Bureau of American Ethnology, Washington, 1932.

Curtis, Edward S. The North American Indian. Volumes I, XII, XVII. Cambridge and Norwood, MA, 1907-1926.

Cushing, Frank Hamilton. Zuni Fetiches. 2d Report Bureau of Ethnology, Washington, 1883.

Cushing, Frank Hamilton. Outlines of Zuni Creation Myths. 13th Report Bureau of Ethnology, Washington, 1896.

Cushing, Frank Hamilton. Zuni Folk Tales. New York, Alfred A. Knopf, 1931.

Fewkes, J. Walter. A Few Summer Ceremonials at the Tusayan Pueblos. Journal of American Ethnology and Archaelogy, Volume II, Cambridge, MA, 1892.

Fewkes, J. Walter. Dolls of the Tusayan Indians. Internationales Archiv fur Ethnographie, Volume VIII, Leiden, 1895.

Fewkes, J. Walter. Provisional List of Annual Ceremonies at Walpi. Internationales Archiv fur Ethnographie, Volume VIII, Leiden, 1895.

Fewkes, J. Walter. Hopi Katcinas. 21st Report Bureau of American Ethnology, Washington, 1903.

Fewkes, J. Walter. Two Summers' Work in Pueblo Ruins. 22nd Report Bureau of American Ethnology, Part I, Washington, 1904.

Parsons, Elsie Clews. Notes on Zuni. Memoirs American Anthropological Association, Volume IV, Nos. 3,4, Lancaster, PA, 1917.

Parsons, Elsie Clews. Isleta, New Mexico. 47th Report Bureau of American Ethnology, Washington, 1932.

Parsons, Elsie Clews. Hopi and Zuni Ceremonialism. Memoirs American Anthropological Association, No. 39, Menasha, WI, 1933.

Stevenson, Matilda Coxe. The Zuni Indians. 23rd Report Bureau of American Ethnology, Washington, 1904.

CPSIA information can be obtained
at www.ICGtesting.com
Printed in the USA
FFOW02n1534180618
47111960-49613FF